How Did
I Get Here?

AN LLP
SINGLES
ESSAY

How Did
I Get Here?

A WRITER'S EDUCATION

DAVID HOMEL

AN LLP
SINGLES
ESSAY

A Singles essay from Linda Leith Publishing, 2023.

Credits: "Shouting Saints" was first published in 1995, part of a collection to honour the literary magazine *Descant*. Anne Malena, a University of Alberta professor who has since become an emerita, issued the invitation in 2010 that resulted in "I Can Do Better Than That." "The Great Mandala" and "Don't Be a Victim" were first published in French in the magazine *L'Inconvénient*.

Copyedited by Jennifer McMorran
Cover design: Debbie Geltner
Book design: DiTech

Library and Archives Canada Cataloguing in Publication

Title: How did I get here?: a writer's education / David Homel.
Names: Homel, David, author.
Description: "An LLP singles essay."
Identifiers: Canadiana (print) 20230229034 | Canadiana (ebook) 20230229166 | ISBN 9781773901404 (softcover) | ISBN 9781773901411 (EPUB) | ISBN 9781773901428 (PDF)
Subjects: LCSH: Homel, David. | LCSH: Homel, David—Childhood and youth. | LCSH: Authorship. | CSH: Authors, Canadian (English)—21st century—Biography. | LCGFT: Autobiographies. | LCGFT: Creative nonfiction.
Classification: LCC PS8565.O6505 Z46 2023 | DDC C818/.5403—dc23

Printed and bound in Canada

Legal deposit – Library and Archives Canada and Bibliothèque et Archives nationales du Québec, 2023

We are grateful to the Canada Council for the Arts, the Canada Book Fund, and SODEC for their support of our book publishing program and to the Government of Quebec through the Société du développement culturel and the Programme de credit d'impôt pour l'édition de livres—Gestion SODEC.

Linda Leith Publishing
Montreal
www.lindaleith.com

Table of Contents

The Lost Pages: An Introduction

Once, driving through the French countryside in a rented car with the radio playing, a suave and cultured voice came on, and seemed to be talking to me alone. "The writer," it said, "is a person who is missing words." That aphorism stuck with me, though I did not know quite why at the time. Today, I am in a position to ask the question. What is a person lacking to make them turn into a writer, beyond whatever talent they might have?

How did I get here? How did I become a writer? What backroads and sideroads did I take to reach this point, a place I never imagined I would be when I started out with the novel *Electrical Storms* in 1988? What happened along the way to turn me into the particular writer I became? It could not have been a complete accident, could it?

I am lucky enough to have a place where I can wonder out loud about that issue, and even venture an answer. That place is right here, in these pages. It soon became clear to me. Writing is about what I have lost.

"The Collected Works," the main piece in this collection, is a true story, and a dismaying one. My father gave me his complete works before he died, a sheaf of a dozen or so poems that he had written as an earnest young man and factory worker. They were not only cries of protest; I suspected they were also part of his campaign to woo my mother. It did not take me long to lose them. I let them go astray. I swear I did not do it on purpose.

After that act of filial impiety, I moved further back in time and recovered a cultural hero of mine—and many others—but who is all but unknown here. I'm talking about Studs Terkel.

Thanks to Stanley Péan's jazz show on Radio-Canada, I had the occasion to hear Louis Armstrong's "West End Blues." Its beginning notes were to me what the madeleine was for Proust. They took me right back into my boyhood living room, in the days when radio ruled and Studs Terkel was king of the airwaves. You can listen to his archives on the net; it just might become your life's work. At least Studs kept his archive together.

There is one advantage to being a sloppy custodian of yourself. You have to keep writing what you have lost, over and over again. That too is a life's work.

Right from the beginning, another issue dogged me. It was not so much what I had lost—though it was that too—as what I had failed to acquire. And that was belief. I stood at the door of the house of faith but could not step across the threshold. "Shouting Saints" is a tribute to the believers, though deep down, I have my doubts about them, and that becomes clear enough in the piece. The churches and the music I describe are not part of Canadian spiritual life, but they still fascinate people here. I am not alone as I hesitate at the doorway of the house of belief.

Behind "The Wax Crayon" stands Psalm 137: "How shall we sing the Lord's song in a strange land?" I drove along the sand and clay roads of the countryside of rural Georgia, following the paths that my peddler uncles must have taken before they settled down into more conventional forms of commerce. What must they have been thinking, what forms of loneliness did they inhabit back then? How did isolated people communicate with one another? I tried to answer those questions.

When I received an invitation to give a talk for International Translation Day, otherwise known as the feast of Saint Jerome, the patron saint of translators, I travelled to the University of Alberta in Edmonton—who could refuse? This was my chance to talk about crypto-languages, languages lost and found, an underground phenomenon that has always been a part of my work, though I didn't realize it until I started composing what I would say. The title of the piece—I Can Do Better than That—is a boast. I have issued myself a challenge, and I'd better live up to it.

I'd better write loss as good as anybody else!

I Can Do Better Than That

Where did my life as a writer and literary translator begin? With this event: I remember a certain high school English teacher of mine, Bill Cantrell by name, pointing at me one time in class and declaring, "You come from a home where a foreign language is spoken."

Probably it began earlier, but that classroom judgment is as good and representative a place to start as any other.

I was not exactly mortified by the teacher's comment, but I wasn't too happy either. A foreign language in the home was a kind of handicap. Picture this: a school full of kids whose parents or grandparents came from elsewhere, southern or eastern Europe most of them, yet no one could own up to the fact—and having this "heritage," as it's called now, was like having a crazy uncle locked up in the attic. Don't forget, this was Chicago, in the glory days of the American ideology of the melting pot.

I remember asking the good Mr. Cantrell why he thought that, why he had said what he'd said. "It's the way you talk," he told me. I didn't pursue the issue.

The guy was right, I had to admit it. I did have a foreign language in the home, and it was my parents' native language: Yiddish. Or almost-native, if such a thing can be. The existence of this crypto-language—it was more or less "crypto" because it was more or less hidden, depending on the moment and the degree of stress—probably marked my beginnings as a writer

5

and as a translator. Mind you, a few other things came into play as well, because if every kid who had a foreign language spoken in his or her home became a translator and/or a writer, the competition would be even fiercer than it already is.

A crypto-language, from the Greek *kryptos,* meaning "hidden, covered, or secret," is exactly that: a language that's hidden. There are many reasons why a language must be hidden; many such reasons are political and have to do with the oppression of one group by another. I saw this first-hand in rural Louisiana, with French, for example. But here, what interests me is not the out-and-out repression of the means of expression of one group by a more powerful one. I'm more concerned with the processes of forgetting in individual and groups of individuals, and how that works over time. And most of all, how this "forgetting"—willful or otherwise—leaves its traces on the way that individuals eventually end up speaking and writing. If this sounds a bit abstract, do not fear. I will be providing examples from my own work.

What that high school teacher said has stuck with me like a stone in my shoe. First as a source of shame, then as an immense territory to be mined— "mined" in the sense of exploited, though "mine" in the sense of an anti-personnel device isn't entirely off-target either. Mr. Cantrell was on to something, though he didn't exactly put it the way I'm going to.

Once you have lived young in and around a foreign language in your home, a language you don't understand, or do understand and pretend you don't, or don't want to acknowledge—or all those things and more—then naïve and innocent self-expression, spontaneous, so-called "natural" self-expression goes out the door. And with it goes childhood, in a way. You no longer trust how you talk, or how anyone else does, for that matter.

Though I'm not much for literary criticism as applied by writers to themselves and their own works—I'd rather leave that to the real critics—I have to own up to the facts. My novels are full of hidden languages (crypto-languages), and those languages always cause trouble, or are the markers of some forgotten (or almost forgotten) trauma. In *Rat Palms*, a novel of mine from way back in 1992 (and praised by the *Calgary Herald*, so thank you if you're still out there), physical trauma leads to the greater trauma of remembering something publicly that you wished you'd done a better job of forgetting. After baseball player Zeke Justice gets hit in the head with a pitch, he begins talking, part of the time, in French once he comes to, even though he's living in Savannah, Georgia, where French is definitely not an asset.

What happens is this: the baseball brings on an attack of incontinent nostalgia (a very beautiful phrase I stole from the world of neurology), which means that Zeke remembers something in spite of himself, something he didn't know he had: the French language. And because of that acting out—he begins speaking French in the hospital—he is forced to recover the fact that he is not quite American, but a Franco-American or, actually, behind that, a French-Canadian.

The fun doesn't stop there. In *Sonya & Jack,* a novel from 1995, Jack Gesser and Sonya Friedman leave Chicago to help build socialism in Stalin's Russia. Gesser, originally a Russian, speaks the language, whereas Sonya, a Hungarian, does not. Through his ability to speak, Gesser belongs to Russia, and the Stalinist system swallows him up. Sonya, ignorant of the language of her oppressor, manages to survive. Sometimes, knowing a language can get you in big trouble.

Of course, it doesn't always work this way. The Spanish-born writer Jorge Semprún was imprisoned as a Communist in the Nazi death camp of Buchenwald. One of the keys to surviving the camps, he wrote in *Literature or Life* (*L'écriture ou la vie* in the original language), was knowing German, the torturers' language. What causes complications and sometimes trouble for characters in books can be immensely useful in real life. And the trouble and complications are also a wonderful source of inspiration for writing—if not the main source, in my case, of both translation and writing. So let us praise our curses and complications!

In my novel *Get on Top*, an itinerant Jewish peddler named Gazarra, loosely based on my late uncles, achieves surprising status and authority in the rural south of the United States: "In proper houses and in shacks alike, Blacks and Whites both would beg him to speak Hebrew. 'What?' he would ask them. He feared a trap. 'What do you want me to say?' 'Say God's name,' they urged him, 'Say God's name in God's own language.'" Of course, then Gazarra has to explain to these good people that God's name is unnamable, and to his surprise the country folk he is hoping to sell stuff to are delighted by the riddle.

In *The Speaking Cure*, the question of crypto-language is both political and psychiatric. The novel is set in Belgrade, in the former Yugoslavia, towards the end of the Bosnian War, in 1995. The language called Serbo-Croatian is disappearing because no one wants to speak the enemy's tongue anymore; it has split into Serbian, Croatian, and Bosnian, which are all the same language with some regional variations. So much for the political side. The "affect" side is more important for the novel's hero, Aleksandar Jovic, who works as a clinical psychologist in Belgrade, which is a real front-line position. He knows most if not all of his patients are lying to him with the stories they tell, but that does not bother him in the least. At the very start of the book, he states, "I never objected if a client told me a lie, or concocted a story for my benefit. I granted them the right to lie ... Lies didn't bother me in the least. I listened to them daily, and never challenged them. Behind every lie lay the truth. Better than that, every lie *told* the truth." Here, the hidden language is one of disorder created by the particular trauma that the client/narrator is telling. This is something we're all acquainted with in our daily lives.

In my novel *Midway*, Ben Allan accuses his ageing father Morris of having another language crouching at all times behind his English, like a sort of court jester ready to make mischief and disrupt what he wants to say. Morris retorts by maintaining that Ben too has been tarred by that particular brush—for how could it be otherwise, since he is, after all, his father's son? A foreign language, according to Morris's somewhat humorous speculations, is like one of those Old Testament curses from Deuteronomy and Leviticus, like sleeping with your sister: the family, the clan will be punished for seven generations.

Were I to re-read myself, I'd have to conclude that we're all better off not having two or more languages, and that having parallel and conflicting languages running in your head at the same time can only be a source of trouble. Not a very Canadian point of view, *n'est-ce pas*? And certainly not a point of view I've adopted as my own in my own life. But if I wrote those things, somewhere in me I must believe it. I must believe that crypto-languages—and many of us have them—inevitably force their way to the surface in an "upward drive of the repressed" kind of movement, and that this process can be psychically damaging for the individual, especially if he or she has up until then refused to acknowledge the hidden thing. I guess that, when it comes to languages, I subscribe to the classical Freudian model.

Going further back into classroom memories would take me to that fateful morning that, in a certain way, put me on the pathway that led to this hall where I'm happy to be speaking to you. One day, our teacher Mrs. Crapple (I'm not making the name up) entered the room and in that irritating "Be-nice-boys-and-girls" voice of hers, announced that we were going to be given the opportunity to learn a foreign language. This news was met with a collective groan from the group. I'll always remember how she handled that reaction. "No, class," she answered. "A *real* foreign language."

Real? I think we all understand what a real foreign language was. It was not Polish or Czech or some dialect from Campobasso or Molise; it was not a language of immigration. And that unspoken assumption turned out to be true. Mrs. Crapple gave us a choice between German, Spanish, and French. German was out for obvious family reasons involving the burning of villages and slaughter of villagers in Lithuania in World War II (not the language's fault, of course). As for Spanish, we had already begun learning it thanks to the waves of Mexican immigrants and their kids who had begun showing up in our schools, more each new September than the previous year. I chose French. It was a clean language, unbesmirched by immigration, a luxury language that spoke of refinement, prestige, worldliness, and all the things we were not. Plus, it was the language of poetry. Some of us more bookish kids were would-be poets, and we wanted to be Arthur Rimbaud and Paul Verlaine, sometimes both at the same time (which meant we would have had to shoot ourselves, since Verlaine shot Rimbaud, albeit half-heartedly). We liked the *poète-voyou* (delinquent poet) image that let us simultaneously be small-time criminals and sensitive guys, and we were counting on French to help us reach that lofty and somewhat absurd plateau.

And here we are today. If you are wondering, you won't be surprised to note that nowhere did Canada appear in our world view. We did not know that people spoke French in Canada. Asking us where Canada was would have been an unfair question, since Americans are not particularly gifted when it comes to geography. But we did have some gifts: all the kids who entered that enriched language learning program in high school went on to become something a little better than ordinary.

That program helped me learn French, and allowed me to become a translator of literary works. So thank you very much after all, Mrs. Crapple, wherever you are now. As I began to work in translation towards the end of the 1970s, I considered that craft as an apprenticeship for writing. This statement might cause some discomfort for people who think that translation is, in itself, an end. A final accomplishment. That may well be true for some people. There are many excellent translators—let me name two into-English ones: Sheila Fischman and Nigel Spencer—who to my knowledge are happy to be working as translators (and sometimes teachers), and feel fulfilled by that literary activity. I was never one of those. Actually, I suspect that even my friend Sheila, though she swears it's not true, is probably hiding a manuscript somewhere in a drawer in her desk. I now see that I came to translation through a desire to write. Since I did not grow up in the English-French vortex of Canada, since when I went to university, translation programs did not exist (whereas writing programs did; we can think of the famous MFA program at the University of Iowa), I came to translation as a way of studying language, and how it was used in novels that had been published, because that was what I wanted for myself.

At the beginning, I saw, and continue to see even today, translation as a kind of voyeurism. When you translate a novel (I am speaking of fiction here, my domain almost entirely, though I do translate some non-fiction), you get to—actually, you are *forced* to—slip around behind the sets and the stage dressing and the special effects and see the very structures of the book at their most naked. The result is often this: a book that reads well, when you are a reader, can be a pain to translate because the sentences don't hold together, there is no necessity from one sentence, or proposition, to the next, the paragraphs are not coherent in their movement from one to the next, the rhythm is like an ice-skater with dull blades. I always marvel at how I, as a reader, can read right past those pitfalls, whereas I as a translator get stuck on them, like a canoeist on a snag. I have gotten caught on a couple of snaggy books in my career. Since then, I have learned to be more of a discerning and critical evaluator.

Of course, at times like that, when you are in a snag position, you put down the book you are translating and exclaim, "I can do better than that!" And perhaps you can. For those translators who are interested in the processes of writing, there is much to be learned, and it usually comes out as a mixture of humility—I must serve this book—and hubris—I can do better than that. We should consider that both statements are true. Just as we should consider that my other favourite and apparently outrageous statement is true, which is this: the translation should be better than the original. That's what I told my French translator Sophie Voillot when she embarked on my novel *Midway*. I assumed that she did not think I was engaging in sophistry or jokes. I assumed she understood that, as a late-coming reader of the manuscript, she had the chance to correct what was wrong with the story.

And correct she did. I had one character say in *Midway* that he was like Athena who burst fully formed from Zeus's rib ... Of course, Adam was the rib thing, whereas Athena burst fully formed from Zeus's head. There is nothing translators like more than correcting "their" author's mistakes. This is a form of revenge that writers should accept gratefully, since it does lead to a better book—that is, as long as that sense of revenge is not fuelled by outright hostility. That can happen too.

But let's not forget that the translator who secretly or not so secretly wants to be a writer can make a mess of things. This is the kind of translator who thinks he or she knows better, and makes the necessary modifications to "improve" on the original work. I confess: I did that at the beginning. If only my author had written the book the way he should have ... Then I got wise and took a very good piece of advice. *Write your own damn book if you're so smart.*

Of course, as we compare writing and translating as creative activities, and the occasional comedy between the two, there is a big element missing in the comparison, like the famous elephant in the room. Novels are not made of words. They are not even made of sentences and paragraphs either, no matter how well sculpted they may be. Novels are made of necessities, the absolute need I have to write this book, to tell this story, without which I will perish as a writer and a human being. The absolute need to know how this story will turn out, and the absolute certainty that the only way to know is to write it. So, though many translators who are also good stylists may think that they can do better than these clunky sentences and limping paragraphs they are being called upon to translate, if they are not inhabited by a necessity to tell a story whose end they must discover, then they don't have much of a leg to stand on when it comes to criticizing the work before them.

In the end, that's the difference between translating and writing. We write the story to find out how it will end. This is the writer's mantra: why do I write this story? To discover how it will turn out. When we translate, that story has already ended. We cannot intervene to make it end in another way, no matter how hard we may wish. Therein lies some of the translator's frustration and restlessness. In my translation work, I "cheat" by not reading the book I am called upon to translate ahead of time—ever—because I am attempting to recreate the writer's experience: he or she did not know how it would end before he or she wrote it, so I want to take that same uncertain journey. My translation is my reading of the book. This method—I am not the only one to practise it; my co-translator Fred Reed does the same thing—creates more revision work, especially at the beginning, but it retains the freshness of the work. In that way, albeit somewhat artificially, I am trying to turn translation into something like the act of writing.

I recently discovered that I have an ancestor, an originator in this practice: Phil Stratford. Apparently, he promoted the same way of working, though I did not know it at the time that I was "inventing" this approach. And so, my invention is actually a form of imitation without knowing it. But as they say, there is nothing new under the sun.

I have wondered over the years, since I am interested in crypto-languages as a thematic in fiction, whether I am manifesting, without knowing it, that same interest as a literary translator. It's hard to tell, just as it's hard to tell what you are writing about in a novel until you've gone and done it, and spilled the beans for all to read. But in one case, a long, long time ago, I probably did turn to a language hidden in me in order to translate a very singular, violent little book. I'm talking about Jacques Renaud's *Le Cassé* from 1964, that I called *Broke City* in English. I went back in time and "channelled" (as they used to say in the days of Shirley MacLaine) the rough brand of English we used to use in Chicago. I quite deliberately turned East End Montreal into the Southwest Side of Chicago and used a kind of "dirty White boy" speech for the characters in this altogether nasty little novella. And I even wrote a preface about doing that. Really, I just wanted the joy of seeing my kind of hometown English on the page of a book published in my linguistically lonely new country.

The casualty of being a translator is innocent reading. Even when I'm reading something for pleasure—that is, not for pay—often a sentence will make me stop and I will imagine the frustrations and challenges it would force upon me were I its translator. And, worse, sometimes I read myself in English as my translators would, having to puzzle out the mess I've made of their day's work. Sometimes I think that translation has ruined my life as a reader because I can no longer read innocently. Then I realize that this process is simply the extension of the foreign-language inner jester that I described earlier.

Of course, all is not anguish. Sometimes there is play. That is, playing with anguish, my own and other people's. I ruined my French translator Christine Le Bœuf's life (my translator at the time) by writing about baseball in my novel *Rat Palms*. Of course, North American writers are always torturing European translators with their tales of that sport. When I was finishing *Sonya & Jack*, I realized I had not included any baseball scenes to torment her with, mainly because most of the novel takes place in the Soviet Union. But how could I deprive Christine of that pleasure? So, I returned to the manuscript and wrote a scene that takes place in the courtyard of the KGB building in Moscow (it wasn't called the KGB back then, but that's another story), where a group of political prisoners who had lived in the United States for a time are playing a primitive form of baseball with a frozen potato. This scene, that started as an inside joke between Christine and me, actually led me to figuring out the fate of one of the book's main characters, who will be pushed from a window and fall into that courtyard during the game, thereby ruining it for the players.

Over the years, on and off, I have taught translation at Concordia University in Montreal as a part-time instructor. I have told my students until I'm blue in the face that translation leads to everything, as long as you abandon it along the way. Most of my students are in the program just to get a job once they exit school, so they don't particularly want to listen to Zen-style riddles like that one. But I am being serious. We should consider translation as one of the arts that uses language as its medium, its way of communication, and in that manner, it is similar to writing novels or non-fiction or screenplays or, God help us, advertising copy, or journalism or anything else. The debate about whether you can teach creative writing—yes, no, or both of the above—is exactly the same as the one about whether you can teach literary translation. Yes, you can learn some chops, as they say in jazz, in a translation program, you can learn how to use certain tools and helpers, but basically the ear and sensitivity for language have to be developed in the same way as the creative writer does it. If I ran the zoo, to quote Dr. Seuss, I'd put literary translation classes in the same department as creative writing workshops. I think the two fields are naturals together and complement each other. I don't know how it's done elsewhere, but I can tell you that at Concordia, unfortunately, no one shares my idea. At least no one with any power and influence. Too bad, because the literary translator's ear and the fiction writer's ear develop in the same way: by reading and by listening and by combining our own thoughts with what is going on in the world, and staging the conflict between the two.

I live in Montreal, a city that is a kind of laboratory and observation post for crypto-languages and for people who are running two or more languages simultaneously in their head. Of course, you could say that any big city is full of people with crypto-languages; no doubt this place is full of such people. You could say that the phenomenon is not limited to big cities with their traditional immigrant populations, and I'd have to agree with you. No doubt the experience of crypto-languages is different in the United States and Canada, to name the two countries where I have spent long periods of time. And no doubt it is different now in the US than it was when my dear Mr. Cantrell and Mrs. Crapple made their pronouncements; the expression "melting pot" is now often accompanied with an ironic sneer in the United States. The "melting pot" has been replaced by the "roots trip," the latter being both a fashion, and therefore a commercial enterprise, and also a quest for identity, a quest to give our identities more dimensionality—to find out where we came from.

But getting back to Montreal, I remember that, before I settled in there—if indeed I am settled at all—I used to visit the city, staying at my friend Ray Chamberlain's apartment—may he rest in peace. A word about Mr. Chamberlain: he was one of Canada's best French to English translators, working most notably on Victor-Lévy Beaulieu back when VLB was a real threat as a writer. Chamberlain unsuccessfully tried to reconcile his native language—his Savannah, Georgia, version of English—with the English of English Canada and the French of French Canada. One morning, leaving his apartment for a journalistic errand, I ran into a neighbour lady on the landing. I introduced myself and, to justify my English accent in French, I told her I lived in Toronto and was visiting here. "Oh," she said in a friendly way, "it must be hard for you to be here and speak French." I answered her without thinking, "No harder than it is to speak English in Toronto." The good woman shook her head at the nonsensical thing I had said and hurried down the stairs to begin her day's work.

I thought about what I had said. It did sound strange. And worse, it sounded impolite. But it was true, in the way that we sometimes say true things when we are not paying attention. I lived in Toronto then: an English-speaking town. I spoke English. I should feel comfortable there. But that was not the case. Every time I opened my mouth, a misunderstanding ensued. One small example: I tend to use the imperative (command) form a lot, and this was considered dreadfully impolite in Toronto. Whereas in Montreal, a seemingly French city, and one obsessed with language at the time, the differences between languages were objectified. The foreignness I was living with and in was clear for all to see and hear. As it turned out, Montreal was the perfect place for someone with my seven-generation language afflictions. A long time ago, at the beginning of the 1990s, in a novel I had a character say: "The telephone rings in my flat in Montreal, Canada. A city made for the expatriate, the perplexed individual hanging between the Old World and the New. A city of minorities, where each one tries to out-minority the other in a comical ballet. Astonishingly, this is all done in an atmosphere of good humour."

And that still is largely true.

Wax Crayon

The loneliness is almost too much to imagine. A strange land, you had no choice, now you are in exile from a place that wanted to kill you and your people and had already shown a readiness to do just those things. You do not speak the language, what the people do here you are not permitted to do, from the food they put into their bodies to their styles of fornication. David didn't know it, but he wrote Psalm 137 expressly with you in mind: *How shall we sing the Lord's song in a strange land?* You go from one lonely farm to the next, if farm is really what these places are. You are not so sure, you suspect they are growing dust, and children, but not much more. You come to one particular crossroads. You have been here before, since your route as a peddler is a circuit, taking you to the same places at regular intervals for your business. This is the first time you have noticed how the houses are positioned. They are facing away from one another. They are having a permanent feud. They remind you of your home village.

By now you are used to this life. No, that is impossible. The impossible nature of ever getting used to it reminds you of the wisdom summed up in one short circular sentence your mother liked to say: *May you never have to get used to what you could get used to.* Or, if on a day you are inclined to get highfalutin, you can quote that Russian, you know, the one who had bad luck gambling, and to make matters worse, epilepsy. Yes, that one—Dostoevsky. Man is the animal that can get used to anything, he said.

By now you have gotten to know the ropes. Before you set out on this journey, others like you who were kind enough to give you their routes because they had done well enough to get off the road and open a store told you how it worked. Thanks to them you have learned to read the signs and marks that other people like you who have been this way before have left to help you. Boxes, triangles, arrows in different orientations, then simple drawings that look like they could have been made by school children. These things caught your attention right away. They were positioned to be visible, at least to you. The people who are native to this country are afraid of hexes and signs and they see the Devil everywhere, so they certainly wouldn't have been the ones to have made such drawings. You figured out what the signs meant with the help of your predecessors, and in the process you saved yourself a whole lot of trouble.

There was the time you deciphered one that informed you, *Pretty farm wife this way*. You laughed out loud, by yourself, on the edge of a settlement covered in red dust. What kind of man in this situation has the time to think of those luxuries? *Pretty farm wife*. This indeed is the stuff of wishes.

Then, over time, that possibility did not seem so outlandish. Maybe that wish really was a horse you could ride. You came to realize you were needed here, and you could finally admit it to yourself. You maintained a certain perverse pride at being a wholly rejected person, and now you will have to abandon it. The thought that no one wants you, no one needs you. The things you have to sell are not just useful, though there is a lot of that in your cart. But there is a lot of vanity in there too, prettiness, and pretty is rarer than useful around here. A ribbon can make a woman's eyes sparkle and she will turn around and look to make sure no one can see what is happening. What is happening to her. That she is having feelings. As far as you can tell, they are not of any particular use in the place you have come to.

That event, the pretty farm wife whose eyes sparkled because of you, for you, pushed you to do something you had no intention of doing, which is to contemplate in some depth your life as an itinerant peddler in the United States of America, in the state of Georgia. A risky undertaking, not something you would want to do after a bad day of business, unable to collect the money owed you, chased by dogs, pelted with rocks by snotty-nosed kids with worms in their system. You have gone from being endlessly alone to understanding that you are needed here in ways you would never have dreamed of. This is a strange country. People love you here.

In the country you came from, the main export was immigrants. A lot of them were of your religion, which was a high-risk one. Here, everything was upside down. It took you a while to catch on. You can read God's words in God's language, you were told. We have to read some kind of translation out of many tongues. I want to hear what God's language sounds like, you were told—and that's an order! Okay, they didn't put it exactly that way, but you got the implication. You didn't feel right saying blessings or prayers in front of or for these people, so you made up some new ones. They couldn't understand you anyway, so what does it matter, and besides, they came from your endlessly heavy heart.

Blessed art thou, Lord, King of the Universe
Help me to understand these strange people.
Help me to sell the stuff in this cart.
Make me a shield against loneliness
As you made a shield for David!

Your audience was delighted. Unfortunately, though it was good for business, they wanted more. Say God's name, they insisted. Say God's name in God's language. Sorry, you answered, I cannot do that. Come on, why not? Their curiosity was blunt and honest. I cannot oblige you. God's name is unnamable. You thought they would slaughter you. Nothing of the kind happened. There was silence. They were putting together *name* and *unnamable*. A round peg in a square hole. They were thrilled to be placed in the presence of an enigma. They loved you. How strange that was.

After you understood you were needed, with that confidence, you started making your own signs. You added hair to the indication of *Pretty farm wife this way*. Blond hair. You used a yellow wax crayon from a box that some kid's parents would buy at a discount at some later date. She was a special woman, the only one of her kind in this wilderness, and you imagined the farm wife's eye would catch sight of your work of art and know it was you behind it. Her eyes would sparkle again, a second time. You were having schoolboy dreams, and you were no schoolboy.

The Lord did not make you a shield against loneliness. There may be no such shield. In any case by now you have learned that prayers are not prayed in order to be answered. They are prayed to make the praying person feel better for the time it takes to say the prayer.

You did like your predecessors. You had a gift for commerce, and you did well enough as a peddler to open a store in Midway, Georgia. Another man took your place. You hoped he had the imagination to escape his loneliness, but it is hard to discuss those things with someone in advance of the experience. You tended your store, you did okay, the *landsmanshaft* sent you a bride. She surprised you, quoting text: It is not good that the man should be alone. But you missed the pretty farm wife. You longed for her. And for the yellow wax crayon with which you drew her hair, generous and falling on her shoulders, on a piece of barn wood nailed to a post. A shame you sold the crayon. You shouldn't have. You miss it.

The Great Mandala
(Memory Sends Up a Flare)

Memory sent up a flare the other day. I happen to know what pushed that memory forward. It was the great mandala of identity politics in the writing world where I work and live.

I am eight years old, maybe ten, in my home neighbourhood in Chicago. I go to the five-and-dime to buy some baseball cards. You get a pack of five cards for a quarter, along with a flat piece of bubble gum the colour of smoked tongue. I reach the cash, and the lady there takes a look at me. "How come you got n***** hair if you aren't a n*****?" she asks me.

I have no ready answer. I know my appearance is different from others, but there are a lot of different people around. I say nothing to the lady. Though I stop buying baseball cards from that store.

My memory must have been out to send me a message. A day or two later, it shot up a second flare to illuminate my pre-dawn insomnia. People who have trouble sleeping, which is an ordinary part of human experience, often curse their insomnia, but they should not. They should regard it as an opportunity, a gift, though that is not always easy. They should listen and keep their dreambooks open on their bedside tables.

I am sitting in the barber's chair in a shop in what we call the "business district," a collection of small stores of marginal viability in my neighbourhood. There is a bakery, a cleaner's, a grocery, a coffee place, an all-purpose repair shop. My parents have left me there so they can do their grocery shopping in peace. It must be some such expedient, since I have never sat in this chair before, and I have no connection to the barber. As he is running his clippers over my head—my mother calls this "a regular boy's haircut"—a noisy bunch of Black kids a little older than I am careen past on the sidewalk like balls in a pinball machine, bouncing off the barber's plate glass window. The window shivers. The barber looks up. "Spades," he curses. "I hate them. No spade'll ever sit in this chair." He brings his clippers close to my ear. "I hate spades. And I hate Jews too. If I ever had a Jew in this chair, I don't know what I'd do."

The ordeal ends. My parents come and get me. The barber takes one look at them as they take out the money to pay, and he understands. What is obvious in my parents' features is as yet unformed in mine. He has just suffered the predicament he promised himself, and me, that he would never have to face.

I do not go back to that barber. And I have had long hair ever since.

Of course, I keep my mouth shut about what the man said to me. My parents, absorbed by their own troubles—unemployment, unruly boys competing with their father for emotional supremacy in the house—did not notice the frostiness in the air in the barbershop. By not saying anything to my parents or anyone else, I accept the shame of being who I am. I don't learn that until years later, quite a few, actually. If you don't speak out immediately, take the challenge and be prepared to fight, then you absorb the hatred and the shame. You become a victim. Of the barber, and the uncourageous person you are. I'm not a scared boy anymore. I love conflict. I can go back and rewrite history, talk back to the lady at the cash, and the bigot barber with his buzzing clippers. But wait—I don't have to. There are plenty of opportunities in the present with such people. There is no shortage of supply.

I know what is behind these two memories. It is the process of my deracialization. Over the last years, beginning in the 1990s, and intensifying lately, I have undergone a transformation that has come from the outside. I have moved from being a member of a minority that was treated with contempt at best, and murdered at worse, to being an oppressor. I have become white. Or White. Funny: in the 1960s in the United States, progressive scientists worked their behinds off to debunk the very idea of race, and that there could be a "white" race and a "black" race in America or anywhere else. And now the retrograde, scientifically discredited concept of race is back with a vengeance.

On better days, like the day I wrote this, that is a source of some bemusement.

On less favourable days, I boil into a rage because the formative and painful experiences of my childhood have been denied and erased by my deracialization. Those traumatic experiences and others like them—I have limited myself to two—have no social value in the current identity politics of this country, especially in the arts, where I can be found.

I am not so self-centered as to compare a couple of local bigots with the mass, organized kidnapping of children from Indigenous families, and the delivering of those kids to hungry priests. Then what is my issue?

Simply that no culture, including mine, has a monopoly on suffering, and that the groups of citizens who make up this society, and who see themselves as having a gripe, as we all do, should listen more closely to one another. A nice platitude, wouldn't you say?

I was struck recently by the reaction of an Indigenous person with whom I was on an arts jury. This individual was talking about stories, and how certain people in his group had the right to tell these stories, and others did not, though they all belonged to the same group. I pointed out that this attitude was in sharp contrast to the one promoted by my culture. And since I have said these words many, many times in my life, and have savoured them for what they have come to mean to me as a writer, I was able to recite them to him, sacred speech flowing in the dreary office building: "Whoever enlarges upon the tale of the outgoing from Egypt, that one merits praise."

The person I was working with stared at me in complete disbelief, then looked away, and busied himself with the files we were considering. What my people believe, which does not necessarily contradict his beliefs, but does compete with them as a way of being in the world, was of no interest to him. Strange, since the Book of Exodus is hardly the most obscure cultural artefact we have. It is shared by many, and was richly and strategically used by African-Americans during the civil rights struggles of the 1960s that continue to this day.

The Haitian-Canadian writer Dany Laferrière called it "The Great Mandala of the Western World" in the first book of his that I translated. He was speaking in his usual humorous way about the changing fashions in race and ethnicity. The validity of certain groups come and go, he was pointing out. (Remember, Laferrière is the cheeky guy who called one of his novels *I am a Japanese Writer*.) Sadly, I have become White. I have been deracialized, and have lost my membership in the community of the oppressed. My family members who were murdered in the Holocaust still cry out for vengeance, but their voices are unintelligible now. On this continent, my mother had a different maiden name on the three birth certificates of her three children as she cast about for a name that would get her through society with a minimum of friction.

Though my cultural anger flares up when those memories return to me, I know it will not be of long duration. I am not interested in cultivating anger as if it were something righteous. I avoid the Writers' Union of Canada meetings because I don't want someone calling me a settler (settlers and immigrants are different animals), or non-Indigenous (like calling a woman a non-man), or saying that I stole their land. I could explain that in my spiritual world, there is no land, there is no place, you are shown the Promised Land from afar and then told you will not reach it, for that place can be only in your soul: Jerusalem in my heart. But I don't think that would cut much mustard in such forums.

My anger is of short duration because I understand that what I have experienced is a natural social process shared by many. What is relevant a few years ago is not relevant now. For some people to be racialized, others must be deracialized. This is a feature of the capitalist system. Let us never forget that we live in a society run by the profit motive, and that the books we write are not only the expressions of our deepest and truest selves, but also goods for sale. The books written by the most socially relevant people are the ones that will move most quickly off the shelves—not that many of us are getting rich, no matter who we are.

Then there is this: if I lose my status as a racialized individual, I might end up freer to move onto something new. I wrote *Sonya & Jack* in 1995, a novel about Jewish dissidents in Stalin's Soviet Union—not exactly a comedy, though I still claim it features a happy ending. I wrote *The Fledglings* in 2014 about a gangster in the family, and his unhappy daughter, who was my mother's cousin and best friend. Maybe enough is enough. Maybe it's time to build on other subjects and other identities, always a good thing for a writer. And for that, I will thank my deracialization.

When memory sent up that first flare about the boy with the funny hair who goes to buy baseball cards, I did not linger long on the offence dealt by that woman at the cash who no doubt has departed this world long ago. My enemy grows old … Because the real issue is always somewhere else, away from where you thought it was, especially if you are a writer.

I asked myself the more fertile question. *Where did I get that quarter? How did a kid like me get his hands on twenty-five cents? Twenty-five cents was big money back then.*

When you ask the fertile question, the answers are quick in coming. I immediately remembered Miss Coyle. In a second, my spirit abandoned that unpleasant memory, and the comment about my appearance that long ago I gave up trying to do anything about. We cannot live on the nourishment provided by insults of the past. As a novelist, my job is to be attentive to the world beyond the offence.

Miss Coyle was one of those "widow women" living in her little bungalow down the block. All single women were called widows on our street, perhaps our society's way of dealing with unmarried, adult, childless females. I pulled weeds for her for twenty-five cents an hour, plus a glass of lemonade. She would bring the glass outside, since I was not allowed inside her house. It was not me in particular. A kid would simply not enter a widow woman's house. I pictured Miss Coyle as she appeared to me once, in the company of a man who was driving her home. She got out of the car and stared at me as if she didn't understand what I was doing there, on my hands and knees on her grass. Then she burst out giggling like an embarrassed schoolgirl. "I've been to the horse-pistol!" she announced loudly. Then she disappeared into the house with her gentleman friend.

Something had happened, but I didn't know what. Something forbidden. I was a boy, and I had been given a glimpse into the adult world. Miss Coyle had gone completely out of character. *Something happened,* the baby writer in me realized, *and you must find out what it was.* I had a pretty good start. "Horse-pistol," I understood, was her euphemism for "hospital."

I had not thought of that scene with Miss Coyle for nearly sixty years. The entire street with its landscape and characters flooded back to me. Thank you, bigot lady at the cash, for that gift. Thank you, all those who have deracialized me and given me the opportunity to move on and be attentive to new things. True, I could keep on working on the old identity, and return to the same complaints, and say that back then, on Miss Coyle's street, my father had had to use a go-between to buy a house because the real estate agents teamed up with the residents to keep certain kinds of people out of the neighbourhood by refusing to rent or sell to them. The illegal but common practice was called the "restrictive covenant," and I didn't find out about it until 2015, after my mother died, and a few secrets got aired out.

But you know what? I'm tired of being that boy in those two memories. These days I'm more interested in Miss Coyle, the widow woman, and her secret life, something far beyond the politics of my identity.

"Don't Be a Victim"

A typical after-school session in the Goodman Avenue School playground, circa early 1960s. Cold weather had moved in, December, but not so cold that it kept us boys from hanging around and putting off going back to our houses. One of the kids, I remember his name was Hurlbut because we could not keep ourselves from calling him Sling Fanny, asked me, "What's the matter with you? How come you don't even have a Christmas tree?" It was a crudely coded but immediately understandable message. I was, in today's words, being microaggressed.

In response, I undertook an act of self-advocacy, again in today's words. I slipped my left leg behind him and pushed him hard. It was a patented playground move. He fell backward and hit his head on the asphalt. Asphalt, not concrete—I didn't want to do too much damage. I was just looking to perform an act of self-representation and answer his microaggression by boosting my self-assertion. I was also out to correct a certain education I had received in my home.

This was what I was out to correct, or deny, if you like. Not long before that playground event, my father opened a book for me in our living room. "These are your people," he told me. I looked. He was not much for family. If he could have gotten away with claiming he had none he would have, so I examined the picture in search of possible resemblances. On the page, I saw the black-and-white photos now familiar to everyone who has wanted to, or had to, look into the subject, but it was shocking to the child I was. It should be shocking to every human being of any age. The *Night and Fog* imagery of Alain Resnais, the concentration camp corpses piled up like stacks of wood. Through their mass death, they had become non-persons.

I certainly did not want to belong to those people. They were a victim race. I was an American boy, and one of the pillars of American identity at the time was that we always win, we triumph. Add the young male identity to that and I was someone who very much wanted to come out on top.

My father added nothing further to the story that the pictures told, and I did not ask him to. No historical facts, no definition of *your people*. No explanation either of how something like that had gotten into the house, especially in a format that resembled a coffee table book. In today's language, I could call what he did a microaggression, only backward. He was not trying to exclude me from a larger, dominant group by pointing out my differences that kept me out of the desirable, privileged class. He was hoping to enroll me in a smaller, infinitely less attractive community. And I wasn't having it. Hence, my need for that flash of self-advocacy in the playground.

I had no awareness of any of this at the time. Recently, I read through a catalogue of behaviours that have been labelled as microaggressions. It pretty much sounded like what everyone experiences when they live in society. Those of us who dealt with microaggressions as kids had to sharpen our sense of judgment. What was a petty insult, a Hurlbut kind of thing to say, and what was an actual threat of violence? It was important to recognize the difference. If not, you could get into a lot of unnecessary playground fights. You'd get a reputation as an animal.

Jump forward a few years to high school. The same neighbourhood, more or less the same kids. By then the boys had developed this little joke. It came back to me not long ago, urged forward out of hiding by the new forms of social engineering that we're seeing in our institutions, and that have spread outward into all sorts of circles. "Don't be a victim," we'd tell one another after we broke camp late Friday afternoon to go back home. Whenever I heard those encouraging words, I thought back to those black-and-white atrocity photographs my father showed me. That was one kind of historical victimhood on offer, but there had to be others. There must have been things happening in the houses in the neighbourhood that did not have a relationship to the concentration camps. Other forms of victimhood that could visit a boy. I realize that now.

It was an odd sort of sign-off. A jocular wish between the guys, something like *Hope you get laid this weekend.* Something boys hoped for one another, and hoped would happen to them. Only, again, backward. *Don't be a victim.*

The victim story returned to me, that odd wish we wished each another, because of certain events in our universities—but not just inside those quiet, genteel halls. Certain people who are not being microaggressed because they are not part of a microaggressable group are claiming microaggressed status. Why? Because there is prestige and pride in being a victim? My head spins …

I have investigated the issue. This behaviour, it turns out, is not some kind of historical masochism or the theft of another person's or group's identity. It is an issue of allyship. This is the new word for *support*, in which, for example, a so-called White person (whatever "white" means) assumes the position of a not-White person in order to protest and fend off microaggressions. I do not think the not-White people need this help. They have been doing this sort of thing for a long, long time, and they are very good at it. After all, more than fifty years ago, the man who first coined the term microaggression, psychiatrist and professor Chester Pierce, was African-American.

And there is nothing new about this kind of support. When I was eight years old, my parents took me on Civil Rights marches and demonstrations. At age eight, I was already an ally of the Black folks' struggles, a prematurely "woke" person. These were also social occasions: we were with like-minded people. If you're not getting tear-gassed, a demonstration can be a pleasant occasion.

As I scanned that catalogue of small aggressions, I fell into a fantasy. A socio-historical fantasy. What would my life have been like if, instead of performing the act of self-advocacy that I did with the Hurlbut kid, I simply took him aside and explained to him the nature of the microaggression he had directed against me, and made him see the error of his ways? Empathy with my situation as a kid who did not have a Christmas tree would have suddenly overtaken him as if on the road to Damascus, and he would have never repeated that or any other insult based on class, religion, colour, etc., aimed at me or anyone else.

Yes, a fantasy. But not a very good one. It would have created a dystopia: a world without aggression. Behind all this revamping of society is the issue of aggression and anxiety. I have a good friend who is a psychiatrist, and he told me a psychiatrist joke that may seem in bad taste at first, as many good jokes appear to be. My friend—we'll call him Bob—was praising Zoom as a tool for long-distance therapy when a colleague of his—let's call her Peggy—interrupted him. "I hate Zoom for therapy, and before Zoom I hated Skype." Bob wanted to know why she was so adamant. "Because how can I rape and murder my patient if we are not in the same room together?" Peggy demanded.

I told you it might sound in bad taste. But the point is real, and worth considering. If we cannot confront our aggression and our anxieties about our aggression, how shall we make progress as human beings? If we cannot face other people's aggression, how shall we develop our personalities, our resilience, how shall we learn about our enemies and what motivates them?

Idly turning the pages of the microaggression catalogue, I wondered if it would have been a solace, as a younger person, to have that name for the things that I and just about everyone else experienced. If I gave the thing a name, I could objectify it, I could expel it from my being. I would have had less pain. It came to me—I would have been an entirely different person. Perhaps I would have been a gentler, more temperate sort of man. I certainly would not have become a writer.

Being a writer means manipulating your readers' expectations, and surprising them. The recent common practice designed to avoid aggression (my creative writing students at Concordia University do this as a matter of course), which is to add trigger warnings to their works, seems in direct opposition to what writers should do. I will not show my most powerful cards ahead of time, and tip my hand. Is a piece of fiction a safe space? I don't think so. Anything can happen to anyone at any time. It's called "plot."

A few years ago, I found an unexpected ally in the American author and intellectual Sarah Schulman. I say unexpected, since she is known for her public identity as a lesbian, but that just goes to show you: allies are everywhere. Her insistence on separating conflict from accusations of abuse is enlightening. Her book has a rather clunky title: *Conflict Is Not Abuse* (Arsenal Pulp Press, 2016). But she recognizes that conflict is a necessary ingredient to social progress and justice, and that using techniques that suppress conflict will not get us anywhere.

And therein lies the trouble with the charge of microaggression: it stifles any further conversation. You make some assertion about who you think I am, I do not agree, I charge you publicly with microaggression—and the possible truth and value of your assertion is immediately stopped dead. We will never get anywhere. My colleagues who use the microaggression trope maintain that a conversation can still take place, even when that charge has been levelled—again, publicly. I think those colleagues are dreaming. It is very hard, once you have been identified as a perpetrator, to have an open exchange with your victim. Harm is overstated, to use Schulman's terms. The people who set themselves up as having been traumatized acquire a kind of supremacy (again, her terms).

I have some Schulmans in my family, though apparently they never made it out of Lithuania; no one knows for sure. Perhaps Sarah is related to me somehow. I certainly hope so.

"Nothing Ever Happens Here": Where Do the Stories Come From?

Over lunch break one day, during the week I spent in the secondary schools, English and French, of Port Alberni, British Columbia, I went out for a solitary walk. I needed respite from the classroom with its mixture of teenage intensity and ennui. In no time, I found myself in the woods, among the great trees that surround the town and once fed its main industry. I was thrilled to walk out of the class and into the woods, hardly the thing that happens most times I visit a school. To my right was a swiftly moving stream. Straight ahead, and curving off to the left, a wide, well-travelled path. And, standing on that path, not very far away, a bear.

The first thing that a city boy does when faced with a bear is to forget all the basic survival questions. What kind of bear is it? How should I react? Do I look the animal in the eye or look everywhere but at its face? Do I walk or run? Turn around or back away? The result: I stood stock still and did absolutely nothing.

I saw that my position was a problem. The stream was on my right. The path ahead wound up towards the left. Unknowingly, I had placed myself between the bear and the water, that was also the source of fish. Lunch for bears, and after all, it was lunch break. "I don't want your fish,"

I whispered to the bear under my breath. I was unsure if the animal would consider human speech in the woods a provocation.

Then out of nowhere, a dog galloped past me, straight for the bear. It turned and lumbered away, the mutt on its heels. The next thing I knew, the bear was climbing the nearest tree to safety, heavily but efficiently. I had heard that expression *treeing a bear* before, but never witnessed it. The dog was barking its head off at the foot of the tree until its owner called it off.

That fast, my fear was transformed. The bear had my entire sympathy. Poor bear, treed by some silly domestic animal, solely out of sport! I headed back to civilization, five minutes away, and the rest of the school day. When I told my group of students about the bear incident, I was rewarded with their bored reaction. "Yeah, sure, that happens every day," they assured me.

When writers visit schools, one of the usual subjects of discussion is, *Where do stories come from?* I told the students in this school, an engagement that had been graciously offered by the Vancouver Writers' Fest in 2008, that no one has the definitive answer to that question. But that many of us start at home. We try looking in the hidden places in our houses: the basement, the attic, the closet.

I told them a couple of stories from my own experience. When I was a grade-school kid, my fearful aunt, my father's sister who lived with us, was afraid of burglars, and spoke frequently about them. She thought it was unwise to go out and leave the house unguarded, but on the other hand, she did not want my parents to go out and leave her alone. (She apparently did not consider her three nephews, my two brothers and me, adequate protection.) With all this talk of burglars, I got curious. What and who were they? I did not know what the word meant, only that it sounded strange to my ears. Once, as part of my curiosity, I ventured into the closet by the front door, the kind of spot where old things that were no longer useful accumulated. The smell of moth balls was strong. I left the closet door open, just in case. At the very back, on a bar screwed into the wall, hung an array of long coats. They were rumpled, formless, *like an old coat that is tattered and torn*, as that song of unrequited love my mother liked to sing went. These coats looked and felt and smelled like someone from the old country had worn them over on the ship. I understood in a flash: these were the burglars whom my aunt so feared. They lived with us, inside our house. That was a lesson for life.

My group thought the story was puerile. They didn't want to identify with a little kid. Stung just a bit, I tried something closer to my experience, one of the scenes at the beginning of my first novel, *Electrical Storms*. It too turns around the issue of a young person not yet understanding a key word, and exploring their house in search of what it might be. A boy is listening to his emotionally pyrotechnic, much unloved father raving on about committing suicide, after which point he storms down to the basement, and rumbles around among the pipes and ducts down there. The boy does not yet know the words "suicide," or "commit," but judging from the context, he understands that they can't mean anything very good. Later, when his father goes out, he sneaks down to the basement and goes hunting for whatever those things are. Hidden on top of an air duct, he does find something …

My class group was with me on that one, especially when I let on that the object the kid got his hands on was a bottle of gin. Some of my students laughed unhappily. Where are the hidden things in your house? I asked them. Where is your lost and found?

But I didn't want to advocate that they write only family stories. Next, move out of your house, I told them, and try your neighbourhood. What might be happening in the houses on your street, or on other streets, behind all those closed doors? Are those houses different than yours, and how?

One of the kids, a teenage boy, raised his hand. "You can forget about that," he told me confidently. "Is that so?" I queried. "Yeah," he said. "Nothing ever happens here."

That, I assured him, was impossible. Stories happen everywhere on this Earth just like the very air we breathe. "Yeah, sure," he said. "You don't know this place."

Of course, he was right about that. I didn't know the place the way he did, but I did know a few things. Port Alberni was a town that had been in decline for some time, depending as it did on an unstable resource sector, mostly forests and fishing. The typical unfortunate pattern in the resource economy of that province. Wouldn't that be the source of a few stories? The slow decline and disappearance of a way of life? The town had three school boards, French, English, and First Nations. Surely there was something there for a young writer to get his teeth into. I kept that thought to myself for fear of venturing onto thin ice, and besides, I was not there to debate with one individual member of the group.

My background had provided me with a gift that this young man did not possess. My parents were Marxists.

Granted, that word has odd echoes nowadays, when hardly anyone claims to be a Marxist anymore. But my parents, especially my father, did make that claim. What it meant in our house was that class, not race or ethnicity or religion or sexual orientation, was what brought people together or divided them. More importantly, what it also meant was that history was everywhere around the world. There was no place on the globe without history. And, by extension, without stories.

I had another gift as well that the schoolboy apparently did not have, and it came from the place I grew up in when I was his age, and how that place was mythologized. I went to an enormous high school called Lyons Township, bigger than some small towns. The school had something called streaming back then, which had a different meaning than it does now. Certain students were put into certain levels, often not as a result of tests or past performance, but due to the colour of their skin or the sound their last names made. My last name made no identifiable sound, at least not to the school fathers, so I found myself, not in Honours English, but Advanced, or Enriched, or some similar desirable rating. Not at the top, but not bad.

Our English class read the Chicago novelists and story writers that year. Before Nelson Algren got famous slumming it in Simone de Beauvoir's bed, he was more famous as a tough-guy Chicago writer. "How the Devil Came Down Division Street" from *The Neon Wilderness* was one we liked. (You can listen to him talking to Studs Terkel about the story in 1959.) In my neighbourhood, if you had the curiosity, you could go over to Division Street and see the places the Devil undertakes to visit, "the forest of furnished rooms," as the writer called it. You can image the chaos that visit caused.

Along with Algren, there was Hemingway, of course, with his genius short stories. Gangsters come to shoot a short-order cook in some nowhere town. We had diversity back then too. We read women from the plains of Nebraska like Willa Cather of "Paul's Case," a piece about suicide that might not make it past the school censors these days. And we were also enchanted by the Poet Laureate of Illinois, Gwendolyn Brooks, with her "We Real Cool"—a poem could be made of words said that way! Listen to that poem read aloud and you're listening to the precursor of hip-hop.

That was the wonderfully important lesson from that year's high school class. Our neighbourhood, and the ones around it, were the stuff of letters. You could win the Nobel Prize with the subjects and the language of the place you lived in. That street corner, that train stop—that was where writing lived. No one could say, "Nothing ever happens here," where I came from. I was lucky to have been born there, but the way our teachers handled the place was crucial, too, for they invited this little old Black woman named Miss Brooks into our classroom. She reminded me of my mother in her demeanour and her dress. When, later, I read her poem about abortion, I realized how deep she went.

Strange, but years before that boy in the Port Alberni classroom, I had an acquaintance with a similar point of view. I remember his name as being Dennis Corcoran, though I couldn't swear to it, not with the way memory plays games. Anyway, I do remember very clearly a disagreement we had. He maintained that you could not write a good story in Canada. All the good ones, he said, took place in the difficult countries. He rattled off a list: Guatemala, Czechoslovakia, South Africa (you can see how far back this debate goes). There were no good stories here. We still hear, though less often, Dennis's point of view. Canada is the place where nothing ever happens. A blessing for you, people from the difficult countries would have told him. That was the typical way of thinking in the 1970s with our inferiority regarding the Americans. The Yanks seemed to have the upper hand when it came to the big stories. Much of the "decolonization" movement is dedicated to proving that Canada is indeed a place with a history like other places; we are no more virtuous than anyone else.

I protested, he retorted, and our evening ended unresolved, though not in a hostile fashion. On the way home, I challenged myself. If Canada, more specifically Toronto, where I was briefly living at the time, was a place of stories, what were they? And, more importantly, what was my place in history? What was my story? Prove your point, I demanded of myself. And that was when, weaving down Bloor Street from the Blue Cellar Room towards my apartment above a Hungarian restaurant, the answer presented itself to me in utter clarity, fully formed. I saw, there before me, the grade-school nuclear bomb drills from the days of the Cuban Missile Crisis.

I knew I had it. I just had to believe in myself enough to start working on it. That took a while.

And I suppose I had another gift, a third gift, one that the Port Alberni teenager didn't have either. I was a Jew. Not a very religious one, but enough to have been schooled in the great stories. Walking sticks turning into brazen serpents, voices emerging from burning bushes that are not consumed, great downpours of frogs falling out of the skies, pure places made impure by our enemies, then purified again with the help of a guerilla fighter named Judah the Maccabee—you name it. Not only are there some wonderful tales that use fabulous props, but there is a tradition of embroidering, interpretation, stories about stories—midrash, in Hebrew, or inquiry, study, exegesis. The new interpretations that are produced do not replace the previous ones; they stand next to them, and the multitudes read each other and ask each other questions for all eternity.

The recent movements that promote indigeneity stress attachment to the land, to place, which is exactly what the Hebrews did not traditionally have. Jerusalem lives, yes, but in our hearts. No wonder the Jews are so out of fashion.

These days, when the State of Israel wants to stake its claim to indigeneity in its part of the world, it immediately runs into counterclaims from other people who are living on the same territory. This proves too much for the present government to bear, and it immediately acts in a shameful and self-destructive manner. The heroic age of that country is sadly in the past; I mourn that fact. Entebbe stands as its high point, and that happened back in 1976.

So, in this religion of missing things, the Lord shows the promised land to Moses and says, "Sorry, you won't be permitted to enter." Some claim that was punishment for his revolt against the Lord, since in his wanderings, faced with angry grumbling from his people, he struck the rock to make water flow from it, instead of speaking to it as his Master had told him to. More complex minds point out that Moses's incomplete journey is simply the expression of his human situation, which he shares with all of us. Then there's this: at the beginning, Israel numbered twelve tribes. When the Assyrians conquered the northern part of their territory, ten of those tribes were lost, while the two in the south apparently remained cohesive. Where did those ten tribes go? They were simply ... lost. But, of course, they cannot be lost. The Lord may scatter and offer incompleteness, but He likes a good story too much to allow ten tribes to be obliterated. They must have been transformed by their circumstances of exile and be living among strange populations. On the net, you can download a "Lost Tribes" map and have a little fun for yourself. You may well conclude that you are among those Lost Ones. Many have made such a claim in the past; it is a form of vanity.

Hebrew culture starts the kids off early when it comes to lostness. During the Passover service, at the table, to the children's delight, they search for the Afikomen, the hidden piece of matzoh. And when they find it—and they always do because it is hidden in a way that makes it easy to find—they get a small reward. If it were only so simple!

These days, I find myself wondering whether that Port Alberni teenager found his story. And whether, actually, I have found mine, too.

Shouting Saints

The paradox of gospel music hit me for the first time in the auditorium of Gainesville High School, down in north Florida. The Dixie Hummingbirds were there to bring the word to the people. The Birds, those eternal gentlemen of the road, had started out in the late 1930s in that same flat Florida town. They not only sang holy, they appeared to live that way, too—something of a distinction in the trade.

They began their program with "Jesus Is the Light of the World." Not only was their version perfectly skilled in its harmonics, it was incredibly daring, showy, pyrotechnic—a piece of virtuosity. Almost frivolous. Yet it elicited a holy laugh of recognition from the audience.

I didn't know what to think. Their version seemed to attract too much attention to itself, and to its singers, to be much good as praise. It was too beautiful to serve the Lord. It was a form of competition with His creation. The paradox had me feeling uneasy.

But it certainly didn't heavy up the air in that hall as far as the rest of the audience was concerned. After that introduction, the Hummingbirds got down to their usual business, which was wrecking the place for the Lord (gospel argot for delivering a rousing performance).

The paradox of "Jesus Is the Light of the World" stayed with me. In the end, it won me over permanently to gospel music, which, I have come to see, has in it all the good enigmas that the act of making art should contain.

Actually, my conversion to the form occurred years before that, before I even dreamed that one day I'd get to consider such lofty, important issues. I spent those sexually anxious years known as adolescence in La Grange, one of the old suburbs of Chicago. The old suburbs had been around since the Civil War, maybe before, but they really started percolating after the Chicago Fire of 1871. Once the ashes had cooled, the city fathers decided: *Enough's enough*, no more wooden buildings in our town, they're too prone to burning, and when one burns, they all burn.

Wood is cheaper than brick, or at least it was back then, so the people who wanted to build those cheaper wooden houses simply moved out past what was then the city limits and proceeded to create architectural anarchy. Long live the rugged individualist!

Most of Chicago is built on swamps, and the La Grange neighbourhood is no exception. So, it just seemed natural to the White folks there that the Blacks would want to live in those swampier areas, where the bugs were thicker, and the diseases they bore more prevalent. No one asked the Blacks, of course, but anyway, that's what they ended up with, and seeing that things weren't likely to change, soon they began pitching their AME churches on that land.

In French, the word *âme* means "soul," which does justice to what the acronym stands for: the African Methodist Episcopal church. It was there, on Sunday evenings, that I first heard gospel singing. In the days before Dr. Martin Luther King was murdered, there was more curiosity than hostility towards a good-hearted

White boy in those neighbourhoods, and I was free to linger by the church door and listen to the singing, and imagine what it would be like if I could sing like that, or believe like that, or be like that.

I lingered there, but I did not go in. Not that I wasn't invited in. You will never find more hospitable folks than the ones in and around a gospel event. At the Hummingbirds's program, it was automatically (and rightly) assumed, even in that racially polarized town in the 1990s, that I was there to make worship, and not stand around with my hands in my pockets. But back in La Grange, I didn't cross the threshold of the AME church because I was intimidated by all that believing. It was more than simply not having the same beliefs those people had. The inhibition ran deeper. I doubted myself. I doubted I could possess the mechanisms of, and the capacities for, belief.

I've felt the same way around the more orthodox members of my own home religion. Every morning at the corner kosher bakery in Montreal, I have to run this gauntlet. The *payess* flying, the somber, grave, concentrated foreheads, the lamenting over the need to make change from a two-dollar bill on a $1.85 double rye loaf, the suspicious stares reserved for those of little faith like myself. It's enough to give you a feeling of inadequacy. Not of the spirit per se, because the spirit cannot be measured, but concerning the outward signs and convictions of belief.

I was right to hesitate at the threshold of the AME church. Back then, anyway. Since that time, I've worked my way back towards the primitive roots of worship and belief. The love of gospel enters here; that music helped me achieve the gift of belief. I've understood that belief comes from art—from music, in this case. I've understood that through shouting, through self-escape, comes belief.

Self-escape? Yes, Ma'am! It is the cornerstone of art, for the artist and the audience alike. For in these pages, we could very well substitute the word *novel* for the words *gospel music*.

If there's one figure from the Bible whom the gospel singer can look to for inspiration and method, it's Jacob. Forever wrastlin' and tusslin' for a blessing. Deceiving his blind father for a blessing. Wheeling and dealing for a blessing, buying and selling and trading. Anything for a blessing. Even prevarication—a fancy word for false witness. The gospel singer is on the edge of this precipice. On the edge of antinomian conduct. He (or she, though the men tend to be more prone to this behaviour) will use the beauty of his voice, he will show off. He will clown around, he will make a spectacle of himself to get closer, momentarily, to his God.

Jacob, "the supplanter," or "the heel-grabber," according to the etymology of his name, is given great coverage throughout the Holy Book. Apparently, the Book admits and supports the fact that one's quest for belief and blessing can bring the quester into some pretty rough neighbourhoods, morally speaking.

Antinomianism, a dictionary word if there ever was one (but a common enough practice in our lives), is among the paradoxes and pleasures lurking around gospel.

According to the idea, those who inhabit Grace, those who are struck by the Light, are exempted from the moral laws of this fleeting world. The false Messiahs, who have come along to entertain and mislead holders to the Hebrew and other traditions over the centuries, were (and are) great antinomians. According to them, when the end of the world as we know it comes, if you are among those in the know, among the believers, you will be able to do whatever you want, because all petty moral laws will have lost their currency. That makes sense; when the Messiah comes, everything will be turned upside-down.

There is a strong antinomian strain to gospel, too, that has gotten some singers into big trouble (Sam Cooke is one, as we'll see). If you inhabit Grace, as the singer must, if you are moved by the Lord, if you can wreck a church and lay out its congregation in the aisles (more wonderful gospel-trade argot), if you can lead to the conversion and sanctification of many, doesn't that put you a little above common moral strictures?

Of course it does. Besides, what man or woman can give so much, can sweat pounds off an already meagre frame, and not expect some compensation down here on Earth? The great Rebert Harris of the Soul Stirrers called it "the virtue thing," lamenting its relative absence. "The life" is how those people living it referred to it.

If you sing for the Lord, and excel at it, then for certain select times, you are above His interdictions. Happy are those of us who practise the antinomianism of perfect moments.

Lovers are superior to the world when they inhabit the blindness of love. In Russia, as I found out firsthand, drunks are allowed any sort of public foolishness because they are said to be in a kind of childish state of grace.

I've seen such things happen. Brilliant epiphanies on the Sea Islands, along the Atlantic coast of Georgia. Underneath the striped canvas of the tent show, the Lord's music was being played, all day long and into the night. Meanwhile, back behind the devil crab concession, the Dark One was lurking. I was pulling for both sides, knowing that one can't live without the other. It so happened that behind that devil crab counter was a package store. Those who had just enjoined us to take the high road to glory were now washing down their spicy crabs with bourbon and beer. I thought I heard someone praise the virtues of a meaty thigh—and that wasn't a crab thigh either. But where was the contradiction—hadn't the singers earned this reward?

The gospel singer sings for the Almighty. He—or she—sings for himself. Therein lies the age-old battle. No matter what they say, nobody wants to be God's voice on Earth. No messenger wants to be slave to the message. The great Georgia writer Harry Crews wrote a book about that, and he wasn't the first. Healthy human pride makes that impossible. Nobody wants to be a clear channel through which the word flows.

Gabriel, when he came down to bring vision to the prophets who turned out to be so damned reluctant, discovered this fact. Unworthy as they were, the prophets embarrassed themselves—and probably Gabriel, too—by rolling around in the dust with their hands over their eyes, refusing to accept the gift of prophetic vision. They didn't want to carry the Lord's word. Gabriel crossed his arms, he tapped his feet impatiently in the sand. Come on, get up, accept it, no one's ever been able to say no.

The prophets were only doing the human thing. Who wants to have all that responsibility? Look at Moses. He demanded proof. The Lord teased him with miracles. There was a bush on fire. There was a voice. Moses looked everywhere but at the bush. You can't blame him.

"Here am I," the Lord had to specify. "That's okay," Moses said, reacting to the news that he would soon be doing the Lord's business by leading His people out of slavery, "but what if they don't believe me?" As proof, the Lord showed him a miracle, the brazen serpent thing. "Show me another one," he urged the Lord. He liked a good story. He liked spectacle. A schtick. And so, a people was born.

Gospel singers say that they're singing God's word. And they are. But what about that twitch of carnality? What about the skinniest member of the Dixie Hummingbirds with the thinning conked hair who jumped right off the stage in the Gainesville High auditorium and started in preaching at extremely close quarters to a group of handsome ladies in their finery? Each one of their hats was more colourful than an azalea bush in full early-spring bloom. You can't tell me he was only in it for the Almighty.

The gospel singer needs that hip-shake. After all, the music rose out of a land that gave us a ladies' softball team in the South Carolina wetlands called the Low Bottom Pirates, and I don't think they were talking topography. You've got to get the faithful in. You need spectacle. Since God's word hasn't changed all that much since He first issued it, all that can differ is the telling of it. A little like novel-writing. How many ways can you tell the same plot? Besides, you won't be able to convince anybody of your intimate knowledge of the subject at hand unless you've been down.

That is, been level to the ground. Sinned. Otherwise, your word has no authority. A child can speak from a position of undimmed, unsullied virtue. No one wants to listen to a child. Innocence has no authority. I am not going to convince you that I've eaten dirt until I unlock my jaws and you see the gravel chips stuck in between my teeth.

Belief enters through carnality. Belief enters through the body. That's the crack where God's light comes in (to paraphrase that great popular Montreal theologian, Leonard Cohen). The gospel singer's carnality speaks of his or her authority. But it also reminds us of the danger, ever present, of backsliding. There is a palpable suspense in the air at great gospel programs. Will the singer, carried away by his performance, fall over the edge? Will art, personal pride and that good old-fashioned taste for big leg triumph over the Lord's interdictions, right there in His own temple?

I've witnessed it. Usually, it starts like this. Instead of "Jesus," it's "Baby!" A snake crawls up the candlestick, nestles in the chalice, waits for you there. And a very confident snake it is. The vocabulary of gospel is tremendously seductive, and it informs and gives light to the southern school of novel-writing, including my own *Rat Palms* from back in 1992.

Glory is a euphemism for "death." And the heaven that lies beyond, or so we hope. God troubles the waters. Drinkers use the same expressions to refer to the mix into which the intoxicant of their choice is liberally splashed. When a singer makes the audience shout because of his performance, he shouts them: "He shouted the ladies in the front row." This kind of language goes out of the church hall and into the community. Every day, you can encounter people on the street or in the fields, some illiterate, who sound exactly like the Good Book. That's the only book they know, the only style that's available for them to emulate. It's always startling to stop by a fruit stand at the end of the day and hear two people who sound exactly like Isaiah and Jeremiah, arguing over whether a scuppernong is a grape or a plum (it's a grape, by the way, in the muscat family).

The glorious, image-filled, yet strangely abstract language of King James helps us feel what we must feel in order to participate in gospel. We have to feel our Saviour as we serve Him. We are brought out, we are turned around, we are kept, our change is imminent, we're going to wait on it. For a few precious seconds, we are totally under the control of another, we do not have to choose, we have been chosen, inhabited. That's what I call self-forgetting; that's what I call love.

Anyone from the Hebrew culture, no matter how much they have forgotten, no matter how little they may have learned in the first place, will find comfort in the retelling of the old gospel tales. Anyone with a feeling for the Passover—the passing out of bondage into freedom with a little help from the mighty toolbox of miracles—has to dig gospel. What person, when reading the lines at the Passover service could claim that they don't need a little liberation, and a little help in attaining it?

Though, sometimes, I have to admit, the singers get it wrong. Moses didn't really write the Ten Commandments, the way the Dixie Hummingbirds say he did in their song "The Final Edition." And there's no shortage of kitsch. How about Sister Wynona Carr, who compares the Old and New Testaments to a baseball game? Even someone who loves the game has to pause and reflect. The relief pitcher who finishes up the Big Game in the ninth inning is—you guessed it—John of the Revelations, the last book in the Book.

And there's plenty of clowning, playing the fool. You've got to tickle the audience, get them in, keep them there, make them come back. During a particularly strenuous show, the Five Blind Boys (the ones from Alabama, not Mississippi), being way past retirement age and still shouting, were wrestled into their chairs by their handler for a well-deserved rest. But the spirit wouldn't let them stay there. They kept popping up, rushing to the microphone for one last holler or shout or entreaty. The handler sprinted over and escorted them none too gently back to their chairs. And since the Blind Boys are blind (not all blind singers really are), the handler had an unfair advantage, and we in the audience hated him for it. The message is clear: the Boys are inhabited by the spirit, no handler is going to keep them down, and as such they are the spirit, too. Maybe they stole that schtick from James Brown—though, if there was any stealing, it would have been the other way around. After J.B. worked himself to death, and was nothing but a streak of sweat and hair tonic on the floor, his handlers would come and gently place a cape over his exhausted form. But no! James Brown was up and hollering again! He couldn't help himself, the spirit was in him. And the crowd went absolutely wild.

What do you expect? Plenty of shouting saints were minstrel artists and blues singers before they got sanctified. There's bound to be a certain crossover. Singing, prophesying, selling barbecue at a penny a bone, getting ugly for the Lord. But woe unto the gospel shouter who's actually caught red-handed (or red-tongued) singing the blues. His soul will be dropped by the church like a smoking, sulfurous hot potato. Ask the Staple Singers about that.

At first, some of us may have trouble figuring out what all that clowning around is about. But remember the Hummingbirds and their pyrotechnical virtuosity in "Jesus Is the Light of the World"—too showy, too much emphasis on the artist's perfection, not enough on the perfection of the Eternal One. But that's gospel, that's its paradox. The Book says you can't serve two masters. I don't know. Sometimes I think I've seen it done.

During that same program, another paradox struck me, but it, too, turned out to be superficial. The Birds were wrecking the church, and many were the hearts that were rejoicing. People, men and women alike, were falling out for Jesus. Possessed, in other words, and doing the kinds of things you do when you are possessed. When it came time for a richly deserved intermission, the Birds mopped their brows with clean white handkerchiefs, politely thanked the audience for listening (half of them were just picking themselves up off the floor), and said they'd be right back for a little more church. Then these same folks, so recently possessed, filed out to the lobby for iced tea. The same people who, a few minutes earlier, were so joyful they couldn't keep their feet, were now discussing their gardens, and what they were going to put up for the winter and how their sons and daughters were doing at school. The usual things any of us might talk about with our friends or next-door neighbours.

What can you say? The spirit is always there, imminent. Your life would be unlivable if it inhabited you all the time. Constant possession is tantamount to illness.

But when it does come, it's a gift. The rest of the time you get by as best you can. The gospel service puts belief—or, better yet, possession—within reach of every member of the congregation. For a Hebrew, that radically democratic side strikes a chord. The rabbi is a learned man, respected as such, but he's not necessarily any closer to the Almighty than anyone else. In gospel, everybody can shout. In fact, you're encouraged to. You're even encouraged to try and out-believe the preacher and the singer (usually one and the same person), though the competition will be tough; he or she is a professional, and you're not.

But whatever you do, you must be sincere. These people can sniff fake spirituality from a country mile. Shouting is a release of the self by the self; without it, life would be intolerable. What with the great competition for belief and its outer manifestations, there's bound to be a few false shouters, a few poseurs in the crowd. But woe unto them, for a church has a keen nose for their ilk. They will be cast out quicker than the Devil. In fact, public insincerity of belief is worse than an honestly wrought sin, no matter how low-down it is.

Since it's the doorway to virtue, gospel is tremendously competitive. But more than the public acknowledgement of virtue is at stake; there is money and fame, records to cut and concerts to give. And, for those who wish to sample it, "the life," the wine and women that come with song (though the prospect of gospel groupies does seem a little unlikely). But the weapons in this competition are different from those in most contests. Who can speak most convincingly about the pain of his mother's death? Who can be most possessed? Who's the most spiritual, who can believe the hardest, the deepest, the most showily and, simultaneously, the most sincerely? Who's the shoutingest?

The vocabulary says it all. So-and-so is a well-known church-wrecker. So-and-so laid out the slain in the aisles. A certain quartet took over the town and shook down the houses for a week. There have been deaths recorded—real deaths. Large dignified ladies have thrown themselves out of the second balcony and haven't always landed right. You can't get any more committed than that. Others have passed on to Glory out of sheer happiness in the middle of a song. This is serious business. This is no place for the ambiguous heart. This is no place for asexual, post-modern cool. This is where the human voice is at its most authentic, one of the last outposts where you can hear it in all its pleading glory, where it can still move you over the edge. Novelists, take heed!

Let us now name some of the great singers. Archie Brownlee. Ira Tucker. Rebert Harris. Dorothy Love Coates. Alex Bradford. Sam Cooke. And the great groups.

The Hummingbirds, the Soul Stirrers (in their many incarnations, including with Cooke), the Swan Silvertones, the Mighty Clouds of Joy, the Five Blind Boys of Mississippi and Alabama, the Pilgrim Travelers. And the choir leaders: James Cleveland, Shirley Caesar. And all the others we've forgotten here. Let us praise them.

Wait a minute! Did you mention Sam Cooke back there? Could you possibly be referring to the master of Top-Twenty tunes that made a lot of cash for a lot of miscreants, tunes about "my baby who loves to cha-cha-cha?" Or was it the Sam Cooke who lamented that he was "a poor pilgrim of sorrow?"

Somebody call somebody sanctified, and let's get this whole thing sorted out once and for all!

Of course, there is no sorting it out. Sam Cooke was both those people. He was the hinge that swung between the sacred and the profane in popular music. Like the founder of gospel who died in 1993,

Thomas Dorsey, he pulled both ways, he was pulled both ways, by the Devil and the Lord, and he wanted to reconcile the two in his voice. He failed. He died in the process, at the age of thirty-three, shot to death. For his attempts, he has earned a place in American popular theology, not to mention popular music.

I wonder whether there's any way but failure and destruction for the man or woman who tries to harbour both impulses in the instrument of their voice, located deep within their body.

Thomas Dorsey chose. He was able to choose. He loved the music and "the life," but he was also deeply religious. He managed to reconcile the two by choosing virtue, and praising it in a new brand of music that contained a spicy mix of blues, which had previously been restricted to the Devil's domain. Then again, it was easier for Dorsey than for Cooke. The pressures and stakes were lower for Dorsey. There was less money floating around; pop music hadn't yet become an industry with its less-than-reputable captains. You could stay in your little "race" corner and make enough to live on.

Those options weren't available to Sam Cooke. After he left gospel for pop, then tried to return to the church, even for a Soul Stirrers reunion, he was shouted off the stage for being a bad Christian. The ante had been upped between the forces of light and the forces of darkness.

Then there was the issue of his good looks. He was just too clean and pretty. Even when he was still singing straight gospel, the Black bobby-soxers would crowd the front rows at the Apollo in New York to hear the program. Maybe his beauty was his undoing.

Some say it was politics that eventually got him killed. Politics and money. A lot of that story has gone untold. Since it's an American story, there's bound to be a conspiracy. Some say it was the Mafia. White folks who thought Cooke was getting too uppity because he wanted to hold on to his publishing; he wanted to retain copyright and the cash that goes with it. You know how those writers are about copyright! Some say it was the right wing. They arranged the hit because they were worried about him going into politics, and about what a politically aware Black man with his charisma could do to the electoral process. (The same rumours were bandied about, albeit less successfully, after Otis Redding's death in a plane crash.) Others held to a theological explanation. Cooke being murdered was his just reward for having deserted the church. Though not all believers wanted to subscribe to that explanation with its vengeful god.

We'll never know what really happened. The official version—one that has never been successfully contradicted, it should be said—was that Cooke was shot to death by the landlady while forcefully pursuing a stripper in a hotel of ill repute. It's very possible that the facts were just that banal. Here was a man who was mobbed by women at his shows, who had a thirty-thousand-dollar car in the parking lot, and who died chasing a thirty-dollar whore. It just doesn't make sense. Maybe that's what happens when you try and reconcile the unreconcilables in your voice.

If it is, then we writers are in a world of trouble.

My appreciation to Anthony Heilbut, whose book on gospel music put the background behind the singers I've always listened to.

The Collected Works

The opening notes of Louis Armstrong playing "West End Blues" was my permission to switch worlds. I was a kid, so I needed that permission. I was about to enter a vastly better world, as wide as what I hoped the future would be. You can imagine that I was eager for that music. I sat on the floor in front of the radio speaker. Very few of us have the physical set-up of a tuner and a speaker these days, unless we have gone back to vinyl nostalgia. Many of us have no such instruments in our houses, and have never seen any in anyone else's. Believe me, this is not nostalgia, I would never willingly go back to those days. It is a longing for voices. Radio is made of voice, the voice is everything. Writing is voice. Someone you want to travel with, listen to, most of all someone you can trust. Everything depends on voice. The greatest songwriters are the ones that only they can sing the words they have written.

In the cabinet a few feet from my position on the floor was the thing called the tuner. You used it to tune in to the station you wanted. In my house, the nob never moved. It was set on WFMT, the Fine Arts Station, so ran their self-definition. Day in and day out, endless European classical music that left me completely unmoved. More than unmoved, hostile. European high culture has always left me feeling that way. But on Saturday afternoons at 1 p.m., I sat cross-legged in front of the speaker. Wires from the tuner fed it. It was a giant pale wooden box that opened out in the shape of a megaphone, and in the centre of that widening funnel was a tiny circular speaker. Out of it poured the warmth and confidence of Studs Terkel's voice.

Studs Terkel's Wax Museum was the name of the program. The scheduling was perfect. I could pitch my Saturday morning Little League game for the Dick Chess Dodge team, get my free Dairy Queen soft serve from the coach if I won, and get back home in time for Louis Armstrong's beginning phrase. After that bouquet of notes, all melancholy elegance, Studs would break in. I was just a boy, uninclined to trust anyone, living in a place where the words *Trust me* were a sinister approach, but he made me feel I could, incredibly enough, trust him. A boy like me could go anywhere on the wings of his voice. All the way to his famed sign-off, "Take it easy, but take it," that he borrowed from Woody Guthrie or, some say, Pete Seeger, both heroes in my house. You didn't have to ask what *it* was. It was everything life held. It was way past winning or losing a ball game, it was understanding that the real point was the infield grit between your teeth that stayed in your mouth after the Dairy Queen melted away and seeped into your stomach. Dairy Queen it was called, though the stuff contained no milk and even less cream, it was some kind of vegetable oil preparation dyed white and heavily sugared, and it oozed out of its dispenser in artistic swirls, and people are still eating it.

The Studs Terkel archives on WFMT would occupy the rest of your life if you decided to listen to all of them, and I recommend you do. There is no better way to spend a life. Terkel popularized oral history. Some say he invented it. In other words, he got people to talk about what they did. Most of what they did was work, or try to, and looking for work was the hardest job in the world. There was no dark alley he wouldn't go down. Work, what people had to do for a living, was sacred. The working men and women were sacred. Very rarely did Studs Terkel talk to anyone who actually liked what they did for a living. That was a powerful negative lesson on the radio, and I was all ears.

When I talk to groups of school kids, eight or ten or twelve years old, and I used to do this pretty often, I would always get the same question about childhood, and it was a good one. Why did you want to write books? When did you start wanting to do that? The first times, I answered in the usual clichéd way. I talked self-expression and wanting to communicate with people, all that noble, educational, humanist stuff. Then I reached back and found the real answer. It's one I can act out in a classroom. Here is how I do it.

I go over to the classroom door. The kids are surprised, wary. This is what I saw five days a week all during the time I was growing up, when I was your age, I tell them and their teacher. I keep my eyes on the teacher; she will have to deal with the echoes of what I am doing in the coming days and weeks. In front of the gaping kids, I turn into my father. I drag my ass across the living room. I scuff my feet. I grumble. My boss is a rat, I tell the world at large as if it were listening, as if it had not heard it all before. My boss is a stupid barking mutt.

(The language my father used was a good bit rougher, you can imagine, but I'm in a school.) My boss is a cockroach that needs stomping on real bad.

Then I step out of character, become myself again, as best as I can, and tell the class, "When I was a kid your age, I didn't want to be a race car driver or a football quarterback or any of those other boy things. I wanted to be someone who didn't have a boss. Can you blame me?" That's why I wanted to write books, and why I still do, I say to the group. Because I don't have a boss. Nobody to tell me what to do and how and when to do it. And I succeeded, right?

No school kid will answer that trick question. They smell a trap and they're right. These kids weren't born yesterday. I don't let the suspense linger for too long.

It looks like I made my getaway, doesn't it? No boss. My own hours. My way. Right, I tell the kids, you guessed it, I ended up with the worst boss ever: me. Myself. I'm my own boss and I make me work seven days a week, even on vacations, evenings, you name it. The hamsters are always running on the treadmill. So, you guys tell me. Did I succeed or not?

If you can put the group at ease, and make them see that there's no one right answer—not all groups will accept that proposition—then the class discussion will take off. The subject is serious at any age, especially at theirs, standing on the edge of adult life. There are more than two sides to that story. Studs Terkel was his own boss. He was a radio star, if that doesn't sound like a contradiction. It will sound that way to kids these days, for whom radio is an antique. You have to watch what props you use. I had a character in a kids' book get chased into a phone booth by a raging bull. A little voice from the back of the room piped up. "What's a phone booth?" I was stumped. In a time warp. Luckily the teacher jumped in and asked the kid, "Ever see *Superman*?" I was saved, and grateful.

Studs started on the radio. Then he began writing books. He had a gift. He listened, and listened hard. And he worked harder, talking about work. How does a person learn to listen?

When Studs Terkel was a boy at the age I was as I sat listening to him, he lived with his parents who ran a men's rooming house on the Near North Side of Chicago, a sketchy neighbourhood where those kinds of places were found. He lived and clerked there from age nine to twenty-four. He went on to take his nickname (he was named Louis at birth) from James T. Farrell's *Studs Lonigan* trilogy. It was a case of a Jew culturally appropriating an Irishman. Farrell also wrote *A World I Never Made*, but Terkel would not have gone in for the hopelessness of that title; he wanted to make his own world. The novelist Richard Ford was said to have grown up as much in his grandfather's hotel in Little Rock, Arkansas, as with his parents in Mississippi. A kid met a lot of people that way, he or she learned to sniff out and avoid danger, and what it took to get along with individuals of all kinds. Get along with, and get away from if necessary. The thing I would say about Studs Terkel is that he belonged to me. It was radio, his voice and my ear, alone together. My secret, despite the mountainous archive he left behind. When it came time for me to start writing, the first question I asked my characters was, *What do you do for a living?*

Often the answer was, *I'm outta work*. Out of a job. A job was a place, a house, and you could get kicked out of it, someone could change the locks on you. Unemployment was the great shame growing up on my street, it ranked just below divorce. No, wait, suicide was worse. The head of the family was better skulking off to the movies than being seen during working hours on his front porch, idle. My old fear of unemployment popped out when my oldest son told me he quit his job. "Aren't you afraid …" I couldn't finish my sentence. He could read me like a book. "There's lots of work," he said.

I took the high-risk route in my own life, which might seem like a contradiction. Or maybe not. There's lots of work, like my first child said. And I had this problem with authority, which was that authority had a problem with me. I thank them for their attitude. It let me take the path I eventually made for myself.

One thing may seem old-fashioned about Studs Terkel nowadays. He believed in man, as people were called back then. He was a humanist. The human is the measure of all that is valuable. He believed in collective action, and the labour union movement. *Take it easy, but take it* may well come from the spoken song "Talking Union," by the Almanac Singers. One of my sons abandoned a job in part because of the workplace union. To him it was restrictive, and he was unimpressed by the protection it gave employees. Remember, there's lots of work. I belong to three or four cultural workers' unions that aren't unions at all except in name. Collective action seems to have vanished from my life. I am a poorer person now. An individual.

Why is that? My laziness, my atomization, my lack of ambition? At times I like to claim it's because I'm living in a foreign country now, where the struggles are not as real. Again, that is nonsense; the struggles are just as real, and the same, in every country. If I gained something when I left my home country—in fact, I gained the world—it stands to reason that I lost something, too. The sense of my own authenticity. A trap of a word. Every place is authentic.

How do you live the listening life? First, by taking off your headphones or whatever little pieces of white plastic you are wearing in your ears, and that you keep in cases that look like dental floss containers. Someone walking a dog, or pushing a child in a stroller while hooked up to earphones plugged into a device or devices, this is an odd but common sight. What if your dog had something to tell you? I asked a guy in that position. He didn't answer. He couldn't hear me.

And then, to listen, you have to believe that other people's stories, and not just yours, are worth your attention. This is another way of saying *empathy*. You have to have the conviction that you are surrounded by untold treasures. But how do you get your hands on them? You need to be curious. In my case, curiosity comes with a certain measure of social aggression. Wanting to get, and give, too much information. Having a tendency to misplace, accidentally on purpose, your filter.

Recently I ran into some neighbours on the street, a couple, man and woman, both of whom were equally desirable. I don't know why, and how I got there, but all of a sudden I was telling them about the freak show at the Riverview Amusement Park in Chicago. "Laugh your troubles away" was the slogan of the place. The freaks were one way to do that. The Bearded Lady, the Alligator Man, the Snake Boy. I'll let you imagine those creatures. I was a kid, the freak show was eighteen and over, but there's always a way to sneak into a tent. After the terrifying Bearded Lady & Co., out on the midway, I went past another attraction designed to help me laugh my troubles away, at least theoretically: the "Dunk the N*****" game. A Black man sat in a cage above a barrel of water and shouted insults of a sexual nature at young men strolling past with their girlfriends on their arm. Steam would shoot out of the men's ears and they just could not keep themselves from putting down a quarter for three balls and aiming at the target so they could, indeed, dunk the Person of Colour. Such were the amusements at the amusement park during an earlier age that, I'm afraid, turned me into the person I became. A world I never made …

Why was I telling my Mile End neighbours all this? What kind of advertisement for myself (to borrow Norman Mailer's title) was it? Or maybe it was a challenge. Beat that, tell me something about *you*, I'm listening.

Empathy is the skill we are supposed to have for successful living, and empathy has many odd disguises. But we need more than empathy. We need to be cannibals. We have to have a hunger, the desire to devour a prime piece, and bring someone's life into ours and suffer the inevitable consequences. Take on their pains. That is one of the definitions of the Messiah: the person who takes on everyone else's pain. Their *weltschmerz*—that was the word I heard around my house, and sometimes it wasn't even used ironically.

In my house, outside of me growing up with the radio, nothing much ever happened. Then, unexpectedly, something actually did. One evening at dinnertime, after one of my afternoon travels on the wings of Studs Terkel's voice, my father announced to the household that he had decided to stop writing poetry. The way he announced it, it had to be a momentous occasion for him. I had no idea that someone in my house could be writing poetry. That that was even possible. When did he do it, I wondered, how did he do it and keep me from knowing? "My fires are banked," he went on to tell us. We were at the dinner table, the six of us. My two brothers and our mother and our spinster aunt Dorothy who turned out to be a cauldron containing one burning, unspoken ingredient. On our plates was boiled beef tongue, and if it wasn't that, it was another part of the same animal that my brothers and I called "stringy meat." My older brothers, more enterprising than I was, would prove they had the right name for the dish by peeling off strips, long greasy strings, from the piece on their plates. They were punished for playing with their food, but half-heartedly. My father, who was no longer a poet as of a minute or two ago, told them to stop, but his mind was not on their misbehaviour. He had entered into a state of mourning, and was getting comfortable there.

Inwardly, I was critical of my brothers. They had no sense of ceremony. They were insensitive, lacking in empathy. I wouldn't have used those words at the time, but I felt they were disconnected from our family. My father had just said something out loud at the dinner table, the traditional place for important announcements, the loss of a job or the death of a relative, and they didn't react.

They played with their stringy meat. Their commentary on the gravity of the situation, I suppose.

Later I learned that stringy meat is made from a cut called brisket. Or, rather, it is brisket. That cut of meat is turned into smoked meat in Montreal, and pastrami in other places like New York, where people go questing for the best sandwich, there are contests and voting and polls on the subject. But you have to spend a certain amount of time and care to make smoked meat and pastrami, and that care was missing around our table. We must have cared about some things, but not about food. My aunt cared about the Bill Mauldin political cartoons that she snipped out of the daily paper and saved in a scrapbook, her way of participating in society. Food is to fill up with, that was my mother's culinary gospel. No one ever voted for the best piece of stringy meat. On the other hand, it did end up in this story. Every dog has his day.

I was old enough to have grasped that if you didn't understand something, you didn't admit it, you waited until the meaning came to you. I didn't get the business about the banked fires. It was a metaphor, and metaphors are part of poetry. They are pieces of poetry in themselves. I knew that much from school, English class. So then, logically, they were contradicting what my father was telling us about not writing poetry anymore. I was curious, of course, but most of all pragmatic. My mother who slept in the same bed with him every night—did she know he wrote, or used to write, poetry? Was it something on his side of the family, like a recessive trait? What about his older sister Dorothy who lived with us in exchange for her ability to hold down a job? I didn't think her English was good enough to write poetry in. She said *key the door* and *broom the floor*. Though that was a kind of poetry, I saw later. My mother? She was too occupied with unpaid domestic labour and had no time for poetry, or at least it looked like that to me. It took me years to develop an understanding of the two women closest to me at the time.

After my father said that business about the fires, I kicked my oldest brother gently in the shins under the table. "Huh?" He turned to me. Saw my inquiring look. "Tell you later," he said to me quickly, under his breath. Like the subject was something shameful, but raised at the dinner table all the same. I would have to wait. I couldn't ask anyone else, someone who knew more about what words meant, like a teacher. Though I was beginning to flower as a student. That was the year I had my first man teacher for homeroom, and I was right up there at the head of the class with the girls. But there was a hard and fast rule in our house and every other house I knew: you never talked to other people about what was said and done in your house. We observed a code of silence. We were like the Mafia that way.

I got tired of waiting for my oldest brother to answer. I looked up the expression in the Webster's Collegiate. Before turning to its pages, I had figured that my father was announcing this to us: once he had burned with ambition, but when the world would not acknowledge his gift, he cooled off. He extinguished his gift; he stopped writing poems. End of story. But not quite. That wasn't what the expression meant. When you bank your fire at the end of the evening, I learned, you are covering the embers with a layer of ash so they will stay hot and live for the next morning. The dictionary told me he was saying the opposite of what I thought. He was simmering down and waiting for another circumstance or time that would be friendlier to him. A worrying thought. Having a father who wrote poetry was definitely a handicap, and I wanted none of it.

Though I was not against poetry, or at least stuff that rhymed. I discovered songs on Studs Terkel's Wax Museum, along with music that had no words, like Louis Armstrong's. The two were allied forms. Studs had a favourite song, number two after the "West End Blues." The subject was a magical escape from jail thanks to a train called "The Midnight Special." Trains often had names back then. If this train shined its headlight into your cell, you would be a free man soon. And who didn't want that? There is no human who is free, and there is no human who doesn't long to be free.

The song went like this:
Yonder come Miss Rosie
How in the world do you know?
I know her by her apron
And the dress she wore
Umbrella on her shoulder
Piece of paper in her hand
She going to see the governor
She going to free her man!

Everything that anyone needed to know was in that song. A traditional song, best known in Leadbelly's version. Wish fulfillment. Impossible longing. A man being saved by a woman's love. What are the chances of that happening to a Black man, a prisoner in Sugar Land? I knew all about *race*, as it was called then. Race meant that you could hang out with some people at school, but they couldn't come to your house, and the other way around. And that no matter what else you might do together, you would always be separate from them, and they from you, a gulf that could not be crossed. The keystone of American life.

After my father's surprise announcement, there was no more talk of poetry. Mercifully, I didn't have to think about what that would be like, having the handicap of a father who wrote poems. The emotional pyrotechnics he displayed when my brothers and I were younger had cooled down, no doubt to my mother's relief. They had been replaced by chronic grumpiness, one of the tropes for a man that age. Maybe the lost pyrotechnics was the fire that had been banked. I guess you can't be angry all your life, though I have known some who tried pretty damned hard. I grew up and followed the normal progression. I left the house, but kept going. I was on a roll—why stop now? I left the city, then the country, too. But not the family. They had stuff worth stealing. Cannibalizing, if you like.

II.

Several lifetimes later, his and mine, I went to visit my father and my mother in their trailer in a Florida trailer park just outside the very pleasant college town of Gainesville. The low-rent image of the trailer park was partially solved with inventive language. "Turkey Creek Forest Trailer Estates," the place was called. A little like the people of coastal Georgia who solved their cockroach problem by calling the pests "palmetto bugs." With a look like the cat that had swallowed the canary, or at least tricked the authorities, my father told me that people who lived in trailers paid almost no property tax compared to those who lived in ordinary houses that were attached to the ground. "Only thing is, a trailer will take off in a high wind," he admitted. "Let's hope that won't happen."

My visit lasted five days. I noticed a number of things right off. My mother, who always claimed she was an ace ball player in her youth and that later on she had earned the nickname "Willie Mae" after the Giants star Willie Mays, had bloomed into a fitness freak. She was either in the pool or playing shuffleboard or going on walks. She was burning with energy, out all the time, as if she couldn't stand the way the trailer smelled—often of her own boiled beef tongue recipe. I walked the lovely deserted forest of Payne's Prairie with her and we listened to the wind blow through the Spanish moss. On the second day I was there, I realized I was not understanding all of my parents' conversation. Maybe I should pay closer attention. Then I got it. They had reverted to speaking Yiddish together, and in turn they spoke it to me, and would not accept that I didn't know it. The language that they had never wanted to teach me, outside of a few rude expressions that might be useful in everyday life, now they were insisting I knew it. Then the worst possible outcome happened. I began to understand what they were saying. I was terrified: I knew the old country language of my parents. What was I going to do with it? I had no use for it in the life I was leading and hoped to lead. To me, it didn't fit in with the shuffleboard, walks in the woods and lengths in the pool.

A thoughtless thing to say. And untrue.

On the third day, in the afternoon, something still worse happened. Worse than understanding a language you never spoke. When my mother was out doing laps in the pool by the clubhouse, the old man came at me with a file folder in his hand. It held a small collection of papers as old and wrinkled and yellowy as the burnt skin on his bare scalp. I thought safety deposit box, inheritance, trust agreement, something I could fight over with my two brothers since neither had bothered to travel to this inconvenient place to see them and discuss the inevitable financial matters. After all, it meant a flight to Tampa or Orlando, then a rental car, then the drive north, the nights in the trailer's spare room with a stash of bourbon and a metal tumbler, the entire place an echo chamber for the work of our forebears' digestion. I was the youngest, but I ended up with the guardian's job. I was not only more available than my brothers. I was more curious. And cannibalistic.

But the file folder did not hold any such thing. I was not going to inherit a thousand shares of General Electric or a piece of the Czar's crown jewels. The packet held my father's collected poetic works.

He gave the gift unwillingly, but gave it all the same. It was a testament to his failure. Failure is an excellent form of education; how else will you get better? By failing and observing how you did it. Beckett's *Fail better*. My mother was less impressed when I told her later, on one of our long, lazy walks. "But you were the inspiration for some of the poems. I took a peek, there's some love poems in there." She snorted. Really, it was that, an animal snort, almost porcine. Less impressed by him, by poetry, or both. "Where did that ever get him? Anyway, by the time we married, it was pretty much over with." "I remember differently," I ventured. True to character, she shrugged. She was not a poetry fan.

The poems were a gift. It had to mean something between us. A shared secret, he had waited until my mother was at the pool and unlikely to return any time soon. And the oblique way my father presented it, that had to mean something, too. An apology, practically backing into it. "Here, maybe you can do something with this. I couldn't."

Often, a gift is an obligation. I would have to read it and react, though not right away. There would be time to prepare a response. His living bequest, my sudden cultural patrimony. I wanted to give him the benefit of the doubt, but I wondered if he was beginning to tip over into senility. Why else would a person make such a gift, wrapped in that kind of backhand presentation? Those were my thoughts, and I am not especially proud of them. Really, he was telling me that if I was writing, he had, too, and before me. He was still my father.

I use the outmoded word for dementia on purpose. This was back in the years before Alzheimer's had devoured the landscape. We did not see dementia everywhere, cognitive issues, call it what you will. My mother psychologized what came to be called dementia. It was his fault, the way alcohol addiction was once treated as a moral failure, not a brain chemistry disease. "He's just such a stubborn mule," she said of my father because he would not rise from his armchair to go out and get the *Gainesville Sun* to read the box scores of last night's baseball games. The paper lay there on the driveway, baking on the asphalt in the sun, thrown by a paperboy obviously not in search of tips. She let the paper lie there. What she did not know, what none of us knew, those who cared and those who were paid to care and usually cared as much as the paperboy, what we could not imagine, is that he had sent a message to his legs to get up so he could go fetch the paper, but the message never arrived.

And so there he sat.

Now that dementia is everywhere, even among the young sometimes, with my socially sharpened perceptions, I look back and recall a funny moment. Not funny for my wife when I repeated it to her after I returned from the visit. One late afternoon, with the smell of cabbage in the air—my parents were like farmers that way, they ate dinner early and I with them—my father picked up my first book from the shelf of his son's small but brave accomplishments. Before my eyes, he disappeared into the world I had created a decade or more before. He was transfixed. He stood there in front of me, he who avoided any physical effort, including standing. The book's first pages contained a scene in which he starred, and that dated back to the days of his emotional pyrotechnics and theatrical threats. After a few minutes of reading, long enough to reach that scene and then some, he snapped out of it. Out of what? He put the book back on the shelf and said, "You know, I should really find something to read." I made no comment. How could I, it was my book he had in his hand. Yes, I could have retorted, "But you *were* reading something," but that would have meant stating the obvious, which is something writers are not supposed to do.

"He insulted you!" my wife stormed when I described that moment the first evening I returned home. "No, no, it wasn't like that," I told her. "Of course, it was! Don't deny it. He told you he should find something to read when he had your book in his hand and he was in the middle of reading it." I said nothing. She is quick to take offence when it comes to herself, and others, too. Not that she is oversensitive; she just has a different social code. I considered her judgment. Something was missing from it, I thought as I pictured my father holding the book. It is too simple an explanation. Then my thoughts wandered onto something else. My father had always been like that. His nature. Like my mother, I psychologized. That is what we are trained to do.

I did not want to engage my father when it came to his decades-old poetry, but I did open the folder late in the night in the spare bedroom to take a quick peek. I was ready. Tumbler, ice, and bourbon, my defence. *Swelling breasts*. The first two words I came upon. I promptly stowed the folder at the bottom of my bag for later contemplation. I had read that description before in the works of aspiring young male poets and always wondered how breasts can swell. Do they fill with some expanding matter like what you find inside of chocolate eclairs? Does their owner thrust them forward in an act of courtship or defiance? Or is the male writer using his own organ as a model for the female body that he may not know much about (though all genders feature erectile tissue)? Okay, I was being hypercritical in my literary exegesis. Some brand of drive-thru liquor store bourbon had put me in that unempathetic frame of mind. But when I read those two words, knowing the male eye behind them, I understood why my mother had no use for poetry.

You won't be surprised to learn that I am no poet. Of course, anyone who tells you that they don't write poetry is like the famous Cretan who declared that all Cretans are liars. So, I will come clean: I won a poetry prize in high school. The best poem written by a high school student of my year. Trust me, there are a lot of high schools in Chicago and even more high-school poets. My work was about the Lake Street El Line. At that age, a young man's heart is swayed by urban industrial romance. That, and this line I trotted out with the girls I longed for, who were just about all of them: "Will you sit for a poem?" Imagine a sixteen-year-old boy saying that with a straight face as he turns another human person into an object. After my contest victory, I decided to quit while I was ahead. I stopped writing poetry, and in the meantime, lost track of my prize-winning poem.

In my father's defence, when it comes to "swelling breasts," it is devilishly difficult to write about sex. So much so that there is even a Bad Sex in Fiction Award given out by the *Literary Review* in England. A very British type of prize. Over the years, the winners have been bemused or insulted, but none of them vied to win it. Yet they do, year in and year out.

Writers load too much freight on the back of their sex scenes. The scenes have to move the plot forward. That is unrealistic. Except for a few first times, which are generally not very satisfying but do set down the patterns for the relationship should it survive, a sex scene in real life does not move any plot anywhere. There is no plot. There is only life, day after day, if you are lucky. All writers should be made to take a seminar, or at least a webinar, on "Writing the Love Scene." What used to be called a sex scene. It is perilous to talk about the subject these days, which is why it is all the more important to take it on. Go ahead, don't be afraid of the vocabulary of gender and orientation and anything else that might advertise your position. There is no such thing as *your position* unless you have fallen victim to an unescapable obsession.

But this seminar will never be organized. In this social climate, no one is that suicidal. No one will risk it even as a webinar, consumed remotely. But I have nothing to lose, so I am offering a short version of it right now. Should the sex scene be on page forty-two or page sixty-three of a novel of ordinary length? That absurd question might loosen up the group, but the issue did preoccupy a certain male critic when I did not deliver the scene on either page, or on any other page of the novel he had been paid to review. He did not find the wait erotic, possibly because the waiting did not lead to fulfillment. Sometimes it is better to avoid that scene—if possible. As a grandmotherly lady at the Jewish Public Library told me before a reading, "Please, I don't need a sex scene. I know how it works. I have five children."

If only we could write our way around that scene. But we can't. Physical love is at the heart of our lives. If not the very heart, then close to it. And that includes all those people who don't want any part of it in their lives, and quest for what they call *peace* instead. A kind of pre-puberty peace without the noisy libido intruding. Characters—and writers—reveal themselves before, during and after such scenes. The sex scene is more than a convention—it's useful. So we are faced with a dilemma. Can't do it. Can't not do it. Impossible. Necessary.

But if this seminar is worth anything, it should be ready to offer a way out. Several ways out, if it is worth its salt.

This whole seminar idea began with *swelling breasts*. How do you describe a thing that resists description, or worse, whose description can quickly ridicule it? You approach it from a different angle. You write about the *before*. Foreplay. But, careful, that is a potentially dangerous choice for a story, because it moves the action towards a foregone conclusion, which is what pornography does. And that's boring. And so conventional, like the soft focus on the big screen as the lovers prepare to … you've seen that before.

You can always write about the *afterward*. Afterplay. That idea is little used. Better chance for success there. It is over, the sound and the fury—how do we feel now? What about conversation? Dialogue, that can often carry messages so much better than omniscient description. How do we look at the other person now? I knew a woman who once told me, "I'm just as bad as a guy. When it's over I turn over and fall asleep." The *afterward* allows you to take on the fact that, often, the experience is not satisfying for one or both actors. The performances were not up to expectations. Or the expectations were wrong. Maybe someone, a realist, would like to read that scenario. At this juncture, some of the seminar participants are probably feeling uncomfortable. They have been there before, and probably more than once. The point when conversation starts, then fails, because the parties understand they have chosen unhappily. Talk about moving the plot forward!

If that option is too grimly common, focus on some telling detail. I knew a woman war reporter who would not remove her body armor in bed, even if she was safe, far from the front. She never felt safe, she was always at the front. She retained her defence mechanism. Here, the seminar participants' eyes grow wide. They never considered such a thing, and how could they have? The props can be more domestic, banal. The alarm clock on the bedside table—what is its alarm saying? What are the pictures on the wall saying, and if there are none, what does that say? Where does the lovers' clothing end up? And remember, they must get dressed again when it's over, and that action says a pile of things, too. Everything says something. After all, it's a story.

Safe to say that my father did not take this seminar. It wasn't available at the time, when he needed it. Instead, he wrote what he knew. The famous male gaze. My father, the love poet. My mother, the object of poetic desire who had no use for it. Two intriguing characters related to me. Suddenly, now, years after the gift, I wanted to read about them.

The sharp sense of embarrassment on both sides when he handed me the folder had something to do with my curiosity. At the time I wanted to say something encouraging, but that would have been an insult. "You can always try again. You can still try." I kept my mouth shut. I was afraid he would ask, "Try what?" He would have been right. What chance does a retired Social Security Administration worker living in a trailer park in north Florida have of getting the poems of his youth published? It would have been like advising him, at his age, *Fail better*.

Memory, that trickster. I remember there being thirteen of them in the folder. I feel the insignificant weight of the pages in my hand. I see their yellow colour. A canary pad, maybe? Even slenderer than the usual slender volume of poetry. And I remember his expectation. My fear of his expectation, more like it: he would want me to read the poems. And not just at some later time, when I could compose myself and draft a response—right now. As he stood watching me, the instant critic. Mercifully, no. He spared us that offbeat version of the family drama.

I had read them. I just couldn't remember what I'd done with them. I remembered everything about the uncomfortable moment except that—what I had done with his poems, now that he was safely dead.

No such thing as safely dead.

I am always losing pieces of the past, which is why I have to make it up. I am a lousy archivist. There must be a reason for that, some deep-seated fear of … you name it. Of myself. Of the record. I don't remember the same things other people do about this or that event in our shared lives. I don't remember my misdeeds or the times my empathy went missing in action. But this was worse. There was no recourse, no backup, no appeal. I could not go back and ask him, "Did you keep a copy?" I could not ask my mother, "Did you ever see the folder of poems when you cleaned out his dresser drawer after he died?" I could not ask my brothers. They were still quarrelling with him, and would not have welcomed a conversation about the dead man's poetry.

I would not have thrown them away. I am too much of a cannibal to do that. They could have gone astray of their own volition. Don't think that can't happen. Inanimate things have a mind of their own. In fact, I don't believe there are any inanimate things. Or *The*

Borrowers could have snatched them. I am willing to bet that the folder is somewhere in the house where I live. Logically, in this very room, which is not very large, a standard room in a standard North American residence, no chateau by any means.

I started by ransacking the room. I sent up clouds of dust. A demolition worker's mask would not have been out of place. Boxes, drawers, cabinets, heaps. The closet. I looked everywhere, but not exhaustively, since that is not my nature. If it were, I would not be in this fix. My eye scanned the room for that particular colour of old paper. That was my kind of ineffective search.

I paced the common rooms of the house. Opened the armoire where the dishes nobody liked were stored, where the mugs we got on promotional trips were stacked, where the stained tablecloths were waiting for some festive occasion. Still sneezing, I went down to the basement. Isn't that where neglected things always end up? I had not curated them. My guilt was obvious and transparent and not very sophisticated, like a dream that did not need interpretation. There was no backup copy. A love of my youth returned recently, albeit over the phone, speaking that word. "We must curate our memories," she told me in a tone of admonishment that I remembered well. I was at a loss, at first, as I often am with words that have changed their meaning without alerting me. I didn't know that this one had come back into circulation. *Museums* was my first thought. The exhibition of himself that Orhan Pamuk set up in Istanbul came to mind. But *curate* did not apply to just museums anymore, I understood from my old friend. It meant *care*. She was right. The word once referred to someone charged with the care of souls. We must care for the past. Well, I do, and I am proving it here. I care for the loves of my youth, especially those who spurned me. But I am less sure about curating memories. My experience is that I don't need to. They are not in the past, they are here and now, perpetual intruders, they come at me at the most inconvenient times, whenever they damn well feel like it, when they know I am at my weakest.

I told my old friend these things. "I knew you would disappoint me!" Then I heard the dial tone.

I searched the basement, trickster memory at work everywhere, behind the vacuum cleaner, next to the freezer I bought to accommodate a couple of lambs that had recently been on the hoof. Next to the sporting equipment, in the chest of drawers whose drawers had no bottom. Just the place to file something away. The poems were not great. No wonder they had not been published. That is a foolish thing to say, and I should be the first not to say it. I had no idea about the little magazine market for poems that were of their time. Hunger on the picket line and the brutality of the railroad bulls and love in the factory during the Great Depression, when against all odds my father was a hopeful young man. The poems were derivative. How could they be otherwise? He wanted to be the working man's Shakespeare. How do you craft a sonnet about bellies grumbling with hunger and the Pinkerton cop with his ringing truncheon? That word, *derivative*, has been the death of many a young poet.

The love poem's scenario returned. It came flooding back there in the basement with the low-denomination weight set. It was like drinking too much. You claim you have forgotten, and then it all comes back—he wrote *that*? The young woman with the swelling breasts wore a kerchief. She coughed from the dust in the factory air; later, she would go on to develop a form of silicosis. The floor boss wanted to keep her and the poet apart, he wanted her for himself. Class warfare with the girl as the spoils. Already, fear of losing what he had not won. From its very invention, the sonnet was dedicated to courtly love. My father was right on the mark.

About three-quarters through the basement, I had to realize it was true. It could have been my father's ghost talking. The kind that doesn't have to wait for night to fall before delivering its message. "You won't find the poems." A cavernous voice, a cliché on the level of *swelling breasts*, but it really did sound that way, hollow and from years past. The voice was right. I would not find them. I would have to come up with another solution. I was leaning on the Ikea shelving that held a pile of road maps. Languedoc, Croatia, the State of Florida. The next move was logical. It was the only one. I would have to write the poems again, myself, out of what I remembered. Funny I said *again*, as if I had written them the first time. I would have to engage in a monstrous act of voice appropriation. Its forbidden side appealed to me intensely. I felt trouble coming my way. A current of delight ran through me. That thing called inspiration.

I felt elated. That necessary moment of illusion before the real work begins. I was no poet, but how hard could it be to write thirteen poems about subjects I already had? Easier than finding them in my house, in any case. The sonnet is a rhyming form and I'm no good at rhymes, but there are dictionaries for that. I decided to give myself a break. I had misplaced his poems, but I did the same with my own prize-winning high-school urban romance. Accept yourself. Forgive yourself. Your inability to keep anything resembling a personal archive might be a Zen act of holy self-neglect.

With that, I got down to work. After getting my hands on a rhyming dictionary, I dove down into myself to a place where a few strands of courtly love still held on. I did what I do every time. I became someone else. That is the elation, the delight, the taste for trouble. Weeks of work, on and off, and finally I succeeded. I am not afraid to say as much. I captured the two characters in the collection. The love poet and his world of frustrated ideals. The beloved he suspected he would never truly possess. It was not that hard to do.

The poems, written under a pseudonym, will be coming out shortly in a little magazine devoted to the history of left-wing movements. Now, maybe I can recover my own prize-winning poem that I lost as well. This could be the start of a new career.

Singles Essays

Linda Leith Publishing - Linda Leith Éditions

How Did I Get Here? A Writer's Education is the most recent in a series of Singles essays in English and in French by distinguished Canadian writers and translators on a wide range of topics of contemporary interest.

Black Community Resource Centre. *Where They Stood: The Evolution of the Black Anglo Community in Montreal*. LLP, 2023. ISBN: 9781773901343.

Boullata, Issa J. *The Bells of Memory: A Palestinian Boyhood in Jerusalem*. LLP, 2014. ISBN: 9781927535394.

Deguire, Eric. *Communication et violence. Des récits personnels à l'hégémonie américaine*, essai. LLÉ, 2020. ISBN: 9781773900605.

Delvaux, Martine. *Nan Goldin: The Warrior Medusa*, trans. David Homel. LLP, 2017. ISBN: 9781988130552.

Drimonis, Toula. *We, the Others: Allophones, Immigration, and Belonging in Canada*. LLP, 2022. ISBN: 9781773901213.

Farman, Abou. *Clerks of the Passage*. LLP, 2012. ISBN: 9780987831743.

Farman Abou. *Les lieux de passage, essais sur le mouvement et la migration*, trad. Marianne Champagne. LLÉ, 2016. ISBN: 9781988130200.

Fletcher, Raquel. *Who Belongs in Quebec? Identity Politics in a Changing Society*. LLP, 2020. ISBN: 9781927535394.

Gollner, Adam Leith. *Working in the Bathtub: Conversations with the Immortal Dany Laferrière*. LLP, 2021. ISBN: 9781773900735.

Henighan, Stephen. *A Green Reef: The Impact of Climate Change*. LLP, 2013. ISBN: 9781927535271.

Homel, David. *How Did I Get Here? A Writer's Education. LLP, 2023*. ISBN: 9781773901404.

Jedwab, Jack. *Counterterrorism and Identities: Canadian Viewpoints*. LLP, 2015. ISBN: 9781927535868.

Lavoie, Frédérick. *For Want of a Fir Tree: Ukraine Undone*, trans. Donald Winkler. LLP, 2018. ISBN: 97819881305934.

Michaud, Sara Danièle. *Scar Tissue: Tracing Motherhood*, trans. Katia Grubisic. LLP, 2023. ISBN: 9781773901374.

Navarro, Pascale. *Women and Power: The Case for Parity*, trans. David Homel. LLP, 2016. ISBN: 9781988130156

Péan, Stanley. *Taximan*, trans. David Homel. LLP, 2018. ISBN: 9781988130897.

Rowland, Wade. *Saving the CBC: Balancing Profit and Public Service*. LLP, 2013. ISBN: 9781927535110.

Rowland, Wade. *Canada Lives Here: The Case for Public Broadcasting*. LLP 2015. ISBN: 9781927535820.

Salutin, Rick. *Keeping the Public in Public Education*. LLP, 2012. ISBN: 9780987831729.